Dedicated to the memory of
the late LESLIE BOAKES.

Somebody said it couldn't be done,
But he with a chuckle replied,
Maybe it couldn't, but he would be one
Who wouldn't say so till he tried.
And he started right in
With a trace of a grin,
And, if he worried, he hid it.
He started to sing as he tackled the thing
That couldn't be done -
And he did it!

1 (frontispiece) Woodcote Hall in 1911. The photograph was taken just before the celebrations began for George V's coronation on 22nd June in that year.

THE STORY

OF

LITTLE WOODCOTE

AND

WOODCOTE HALL

by

MARGARET CUNNINGHAM

Heritage in Sutton Leisure

First published 1989

Heritage in Sutton Leisure
Central Library, St. Nicholas Way
Sutton, Surrey, SM1 1EA

ISBN 0 907335 20 9

Printed by Dasprint Limited
53 Lydden Grove, London SW18 4LW

CONTENTS

ACKNOWLEDGEMENTS

Before he died, Leslie Boakes had persuaded me to write this book. Despite his ill-health, he gave me a conducted tour of Woodcote Hall and its environs in May, 1979, and then supplied me with the information he had collected in respect of the house since 1935, including a copy of its title deeds. My sincere thanks go to his widow, Mrs. Hylda Boakes, for her help and interest in my project.

My sincere and grateful thanks are given to everyone who helped me during the years of research and work on the book, especially to Miss Mary Batchelor, Mr. S.A. Bird, Mrs. W.E. Blow, Mrs. W.C. Bond*, Mr. Ian Bradley, Miss Joyce Breadon, Mrs. F.C. Bridle*; to Miss June Broughton for her invaluable assistance with information from Sutton Central Library's archives and elsewhere; to Mr. Nicholas Burnett for supplying details from his own research work; to Mr. Ted Cannon, the site foreman at Woodcote Hall, and his workmen; to Miss Heather Cant for her help and support; to the late Mrs. Patricia Clark; to Mr. Douglas Cluett for his most helpful advice and editorial assistance; to Mrs. P.M. Colston-Turner*; to Mrs. G.C.M. de Koning*; to the late Reverend Costin Densham; to Mrs. O.M. Dymond* and the late Mr. H.E. Dymond*; to Mrs. Shirley Edwards for her graphics and design; to the late Mr. Farren of Farren Estates Ltd., for information about Stanley House; to Mr. A. Freeman for arranging the visit to the lofts at Woodcote Hall; to Mr. and Mrs. E. Fuller, Mr. and Mrs. John Garrod*; to Mr. and Mrs. M. Griffin for visits to West Lodge; to Mrs. M.J. Hamilton-Bradbury for providing information from her own research work; to Mrs. Norah Hartland*; to Mr. J. Henderson of the Chelsea Speleological Society; to Mr. Ray Hollands for allowing visits to Woodcote Hall before it was sold; to Mr. H.G.W. Hosking*; to Mr. David Jackson for his interest and permission for investigations at Woodcote Hall during the restoration work; to Mr. A.E. Jones; to Mr. David Martin of Woodcote Hall Cottage; to Mr. Ken Mercer, Mr. Keith Page, Mr. John Phillips, Mr. Keith Pryer*; to Mr. Brian Reed and his staff at Reed & Woods, Estate Agents; to Mrs. M.E. Reynolds for her memories of Stanley House; to Mrs. J.C. Richardson for permission to use her research notes on the Carew family; to Miss S. Theakstone, Mrs. Angela Vaughan, Mr. and Mrs. T.R. Veale, Mr. J. Vinn, Mr. and Mrs. J.S. Waites, Mr. Barry Weston; to Professor M. Wilks for his helpful criticisms; to the staff at the Bourne Hall Library, Ewell, and the Surrey Record Office, Kingston-upon-Thames; to members of staff on Level 4 of the Central Library, Sutton and in the Reference Library at Wallington.

Lastly, any errors left in the book are my responsibility, as every effort has been made to prevent me making them.

(* denotes former tenants at Woodcote Hall)

ILLUSTRATIONS ACKNOWLEDGEMENTS

All illustrations are to be found in the Local Collection of the Heritage Devision, Sutton Leisure Services, with the exception of the following, to whom thanks are due.

2 By kind permission of the Surrey Record Office, who hold the original.
3,32, 33 Based on Ordnance Survey maps 1896, 1913 and 1975, with the sanction of the Controller of H.M. Stationery Office. Crown Copyright reserved.
4 Roy and Lesley Adkins.
5 Lesley Adkins and Stuart Needham.
8 Basel, Offentliche Kunstsammerlung, Kupferstichkabinett.
15,15 Surrey County Libraries
18, 31, 38, 41, 43-45 The author
40 Shirley Edwards

INTRODUCTION

A large part of Woodcote occupies the south-eastern corner of the London Borough of Sutton, but it is difficult to assess the exact extent of it, because most of its boundaries were not marked on any of the old maps. After its division into Little and Greater Woodcote in the late eighteenth century, a section of Woodcote's western boundary appeared on a survey map of 'Little Woodcot' dated 1818, which also gave the field names in use at that time.

Little Woodcote was once the estate of Woodcote Lodge, known for many years as Woodcote, or the Lodge at Woodcote; and, from 1875, Woodcote Hall. This recently restored house stands in Woodcote Avenue by Park Hill Road in Wallington. Deceptively, its present-day appearance hides its true age, because the earliest part of the building probably dates from before 1520.

The full history of Woodcote Hall and Little Woodcote is closely interwoven with that of early Woodcote itself, and, therefore, cannot be separated from it. I am sure that there is much more information yet to be discovered about the area; not only from beneath the ground in respect of the earliest-known settlement, the later alleged Roman town, and the location of the lost medieval village, but also in old manuscripts and other documents.

Finally, I wish to point out that the spelling of words in some of the quoted manuscripts has been modernised for ease of reading.

Margaret Cunningham
1987

CHAPTER 1

FROM PREHISTORIC TO SAXON TIMES

Prehistoric man left plenty of evidence to substantiate his visits to Woodcote and, to date, the oldest find here has been a Palaeolithic (early Stone Age) Acheulian handaxe.[1] In 1968, during the fieldwork carried out in preparation for laying a large gas pipeline through Little Woodcote, the adjacent lands in the Oaks Park and Woodmansterne, some struck flints, possibly Neolithic (late Stone Age c.3200 B.C.) were uncovered.[2]

Over the last twenty years, a quantity of worked flints have been gathered within an area of a few hundred yards across in Little Woodcote by David and Robert Stanbridge. These finds range in date from the Mesolithic (middle Stone Age c.7000 B.C.) to the Bronze Age (2300-700 B.C.), and include flakes, blades, scrapers, cores, points, awls, rods, axes and arrowheads. Some of the artefacts have been damaged probably by continuous cultivation of the land, while others show evidence of being re-worked into a different type of implement at a later date than the ones from which these originated.[3]

Woodcote's earliest-known inhabitants lived on its western edge, on land which, many centuries later, became part of Little Woodcote. The site of their settlement was discovered when excavations for the foundations of Queen Mary's Hospital commenced in 1903, and workmen, who were digging out a trench for drains on the low hill known as Stag Field, accidentally "cut through a mass of black earth containing bones and pottery". Thus the site's true archaeological value was revealed, and some local archaeologists took the opportunity to search here until 1905.[4]

Many traces of habitation of the site were found during further excavations carried out by the workmen and archaeological diggers under the supervision of Messrs. H.C. Collyer and N.F. Robarts. Flint flakes and implements, some hearths, charred grain and human bones were uncovered. However, it was impossible to trace the full extent of an outer ditch around the settlement to assess the size of the enclosure, because of erosion by the weather and constant ploughing on part of the

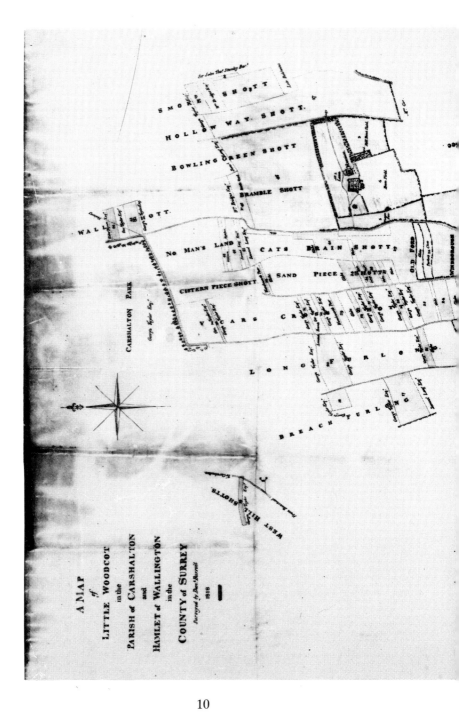

A MAP
of
LITTLE WOODCOT
in the
PARISH of CARSHALTON
and
HAMLET of WALLINGTON
in the
COUNTY of SURREY
Surveyed by Dan'l Burrell
1818

SMOKE SHOTT

HOLLOW WAY SHOTT

BOWLING GREEN SHOTT

BRAMBLE SHOTT

WALL SHOTT

No. MAN'S LAND

CATS BRAIN SHOTT

CISTERN PIECE SHOTT

SAND PIECE SHOTT

VICARS CROSS

CARSHALTON PARK

LONG FURLONG

BREACH FURLONG

OLD FORD

WEST HILL SHOTT

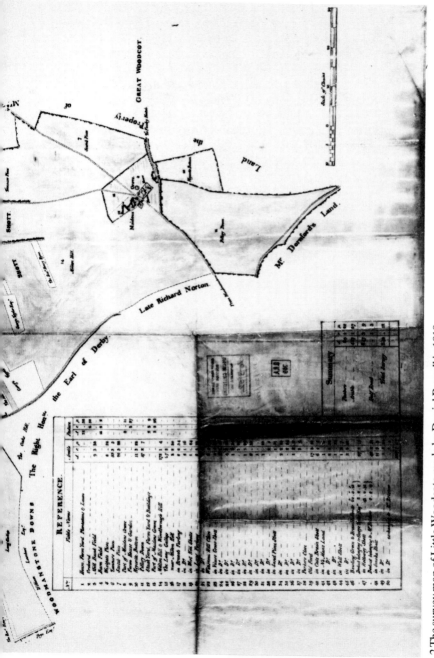

2 The survey map of Little Woodcote made by Daniel Burrell in 1818.

11

land,[4] but it was thought to cover about four acres. Later, Robarts deduced that the ditch formed part of a circular enclosed area one hundred and fifty metres in diameter. This earthwork has been dated from the late Bronze Age[5] (1000-700 B.C.) but some of the numerous flint implements found within and around it date from the Neolithic period; also, a number of the flints and flakes have been identified as originating from earlier Mesolithic times.[6]

The living quarters inside the enclosure were, probably, timber and thatch huts and there was a plentiful water supply from the streams which flowed northwards down the hillside. The source of one stream near the settlement has been found in the corner of a field on the smallholding adjacent to Queen Mary's Hospital's playing-fields. In the early 1930s, the stream's course was traced through a garden in Briar Banks, across Briar Lane and along part of Mount Park.[7] Possibly, the field name of Old Ford arose from the time when there was a suitable, shallow place to cross the water here.

Further investigations by archaeologists from 1937 onwards have established that occupation of the earthworks began in the late Bronze Age, and it was likely that most of the worked flints discovered here belonged to this period, although none had been kept from earlier observations. Excavations were carried out both inside and outside the enclosure and in part of the surrounding ditch. The finds included a quantity of pottery, an amber bead, a ring with a suspension loop, a flat, bronze fragment, a lump of copper, a bronze bar and lancehead, perforated clay slabs, loomweights and spindle whorls, and a small fragment of a bronze sword was found in Little Woodcote close to the hospital.[5]

Although two presumed hearths were discovered inside the enclosure in 1905, the black layers in the ditch suggested that cooking could have been carried out in it because it provided shelter from the wind. Pottery was found here and included an earthenware food-vessel, which had fingernail impressions on the shoulder and contained seeds of wheat, barley, and one of Good King Henry (now a cultivated weed). One large sherd of a bowl, some calcined flints, a piece of a bronze ingot, and a possible part of a crucible were uncovered outside the earthworks, and it would seem likely that this area was used for metal working. The finds of grain and numerous querns on the site indicated a certain amount of domestic and agricultural activities, and there were indications for the rearing of cattle and, probably, sheep-farming. The clay weights, if not used as thatch weights but with a loom, could be associated with the spindle whorls as evidence for the production of woollen cloth here.[5]

It has been suggested that this site was a circular, defended enclosure in the late Bronze Age, when, probably, it was a regional focus with control over a tract of downland about ten kilometres across.[5] One of the nearest settlements then would have been at Beddington, where pottery dating from this period was discovered during recent excavations to trace the Roman villa there.[8]

Evidence of early Iron Age occupation of the enclosure (700-500 B.C.) was provided by some of the pottery found here, including an important fragment of an urn, or vessel, of a type traced to a source outside Britain.[4] Other pottery dated from the late Iron Age (200 B.C.-43 A.D.) and it is thought that the site also had a certain importance in the area during this period.[5] However, the finds from inside and outside the enclosure do not necessarily substantiate that it was continuously occupied throughout the aforementioned periods.[6]

The burial mounds (barrows) on the north-western side of the enclosure have disappeared during the last two centuries, when the land on which they stood (in Barrow Hedges) was used for farming purposes. This precludes any positive dating of them, but they could have been of Bronze Age origins, if not earlier.[5,6] William Camden, in his *Britannia* (1586), said that there were three tumuli here; and, when Salmon wrote his history of Surrey in 1736, he called them "Gally Hills" or "Devil's Mounds". Gally is an obsolete word meaning to scare, or frighten,[9] and suggests that some kind of folklore was connected with them in Salmon's time.

Before he published his *Historical Notes on Wallington* in 1873, the Reverend John Williams interviewed the "Proprietor of Woodcote" and, during a discussion about Woodcote's early inhabitants, this gentleman pointed out a mound in the grounds of his residence, and suggested that it should be opened to ascertain if it was another barrow. The vicar did not specifically name the house to which he referred, but it seems logical to conclude that it was Woodcote Lodge, because he called it Woodcote and the fact of its proximity to the enclosure in Little Woodcote. Also, what could be a 'mound' on the south-western side of the walled garden here is shown on the 1896 Ordnance Survey map.

There has been much speculation about Woodcote's importance in Roman times. In his *Britannia* of 1586, William Camden said that the remains of a town, and many old wells built of flints, could plainly be seen here, and "the locals frequently remark on the number and wealth of its inhabitants". Camden's theory that it was the site of a Roman city

3 A section of a recent Ordnance Survey map showing the boundaries of the largest part of Little Woodcote in 1829. Those marked on the top left-hand side are approximate only.

15

called Noiomagus by Ptolemy, and Noviomagus by Antoninus,[10] had Talbot's support in 1610, when he wrote his commentary to explain the Antonine Itinerary[11] (the Roman equivalent to the modern AA Guide) compiled c.120 A.D. in Emperor Hadrian's reign, and gave information about towns on certain routes, with the distances between them, for the guidance of Roman commanders and their armies.[12]

Other learned gentlemen, who wrote commentaries on the Itinerary, supported Talbot's opinion.[11] A Mr. Symmes, who died in about 1630, said that the Neomagus, or Noviomagus, of Ptolemy was sited on a woody hill called Woodcote.[13] Thomas Gale's commentary, published in 1709, described the route of a Roman road through Streatham, Croydon, and "...up to Woodcote Warren, i.e. Noviomagus". Both established tradition and his personal observations suggested that a town stood there, and he had seen "...many paving stones, tiles, streets, foundations and squared stones; nearby there are also many wells for drawing up water, which are (I deduce from one of them) incredibly deep".[10]

John Aubrey intended to visit each place he described in his *Natural History and Antiquities of the County of Surrey* (1673-1692)[14] and was reminded by John Evelyn, the diarist, that, by February 1676, he had not made his "journey about Bansted, where was the famous Woodcot, of which you shall find mention in Mr. Burton's notes upon Antoninus' Itinerary. There are to this Day, Roman Coins, Urns and Bricks, and co., dug up by the Rusticks".[10] Aubrey did visit Woodcote, and in his description of the Wallington Hundred, he wrote: "In this Hundred rises the River Wandle, and on Top of the Hill adjacent appear great Tokens of an once flourishing Town, which Camden takes to be the ancient Noviomagus mentioned by Ptolemy, of which remains Ruines built of Flints, Stones, etc. Here, Dr. Gale tells us, the Roman Road divides itself into three parts".[14] In Salmon's history of Surrey (1736), he mentioned the traces of buildings here, as well as axes and spearheads found in the fields, and many old wells, but he was not sure that it was Noviomagus.[10] Bowen's map of Surrey in 1760 showed Woodcote Warren, which included lands in the present-day Little Woodcote, as "Woodcote, or Woodcote Warren, once a City according to Tradition".

Nearer to our own times, the Reverend John Williams said that the wells at Woodcote "remain to this day of 1872",[15] but did not give their exact location. Also the "Proprietor of Woodcote" informed him of a peculiar ivory ball found on his land. The vicar suggested that proof of Woodcote's importance in Roman times could be found by tracing

16

acknowledged Roman roads through Surrey, Sussex and Kent, because, he said, all of these converged around the southern part of Wallington at Woodcote,[15] (although this is not actually true).

During excavations on the site of Queen Mary's Hospital in 1905, workmen accidentally cut through a small fragment of tile not unlike other Roman fragments[16] and Roman pottery and coins have been found there.[1] More finds in the enclosure's vicinity, such as a Roman lamp in Pine Walk (seen by the author but its present whereabouts are unknown), a silver spoon from Barrow Hedges, a horse skeleton and pottery in The Gallop on Carshalton Downs,[1] suggest some form of Roman habitation near, if not on, the ancient settlement. An early tenant of a smallholding adjacent to the hospital's grounds uncovered two, old, straight, flint paths, each about twelve feet in width, on either boundary of his farmland.[16]

Not far from Woodcote, a Roman bath-house was discovered at Beddington in 1871, and recent excavations revealed a villa, a wide range of pottery and other objects to indicate that, probably, the site was continuously occupied from the late first century A.D. until well into the fourth century A.D.[8] Two Roman coffins were found near Beddington Church; a lead one in c.1870 on the western border of the churchyard, and a large stone coffin in Church Path on 10th March, 1930.[17] Recent and previous finds at Bandon Hill Cemetery included cremation burials, pottery sherds, and burnt human bones, dating from c.300-400 A.D. and led to the conclusion that these could indicate another separate centre of Romano-British habitation. The discoveries of Iron Age sherds and flints here suggested that the site was, possibly, of pre-Roman origin.[18,19]

A local archaeologist, the late K.W. Muckleroy, said that the Roman town of Noviomagus never existed at Woodcote, and it was the ruins of a medieval village which Camden and Aubrey saw here. Although Salmon described it as: "Woodcote has been a place full of inhabitants, as appears from the traces of streets and the number of wells, some of which have been very deep", Mr. Muckleroy suggested that the villagers abandoned their homes at the time of the Black Death plague in 1349, and, probably, these were sited at Woodcote Farm – now Farm Lane in Purley. Afterwards the ruins were destroyed in the eighteenth century, when the land was used for farming.[10] However, one argument against his theory about the village is the fact that Woodcote's inhabitants continued to pay taxes after 1349, and up to the end of the seventeenth century.[20]

Although the majority of people who have investigated the possibility

17

that Woodcote was the site of Noviomagus have not reached any positive conclusions on the subject, they have generally accepted that there was some form of settlement here by the Romans. Thus, Woodcote's importance in Roman times will continue to provide more speculation for many future years.

Direct government by the Romans gradually ceased at the beginning of the fifth century A.D., and after the subsequent invasions of Britain by the Angles and Saxons, the latter people settled in Woodcote. Some of their pottery and burial urns were discovered in Queen Mary's Hospital grounds, and suggested a possible site for a Saxon cemetery, also the barrows in Barrow Hedges could be attributed to that period.[1,6] Woodcot(e) is derived from the Anglo-Saxon 'cot' or 'cote' and means a small house, hut or shelter for beasts[9] in a wood, and suggests that the first house here was built at that time and gave its name to the village. Later, the Normans' conquest of England and their strengthening of the manorial system affected the pattern of life of some of Woodcote's inhabitants.

CHAPTER 2

THE LOST MEDIEVAL VILLAGE OF WOODCOTE

In the Domesday Survey of 1086, Woodcote appeared to be "generally apart"[15] from other local manors, but could have been included in the manor later known as Home Beddington or West Court, where the tenant-in-chief was Richard de Tonbridge, the founder of the powerful medieval family of Clare. Probably, it was administered by the Crown, with the exception of some of its western lands (i.e. on the west of the old Beddington/Carshalton parish boundary along present-day Boundary Road and the bridleway across the smallholdings), which came under Carshalton's manor given by William I to one of his elite noblemen, Geoffrey de Mandeville.[21]

Most of Woodcote was administered by the Crown from Henry II's reign for at least another two centuries, and a number of references to the village appeared in the Curia Regis rolls kept by the Royal Court of Law. The first one referred to a dispute over a will in 1202, which involved land in Beddington and one acre at Woodcote, and there were four other, similar cases in King John's reign. In 1223, a jury of twenty-one local men was sworn in to witness "what dues and services...were rendered to King Henry, the grandfather of the lord King, and Richard, his uncle, from the lands they held in Waleton and Woodcot...", and Alured and Gilbert de Wodecot were among the jurors.[10] After 1228, part of Woodcote's land was granted to St. Thomas's Hospital in Southwark.[22]

Some old documents discovered recently in the British Library refer to leases of small pieces of land in Bandon, Beddington, Wallington and Woodcote from Edward I's reign (1272-1307) onwards. The names of people concerned in these transactions, and the witnesses to them, were given, and William le Glenge; William Baudri; Thomas, son of Alured; Galdricus le Hole, who held property in Beddington; Baldrus; Wymores; Galfridus and his son, Simon, were among Woodcote's inhabitants at that time.[23]

William, son of Baldrus de Wodecot, gave two acres of his land in East Woodcote to Walter de Rokesle, and one of these was situated "on both sides and bordering upon Grenestrete towards the Court of the Rector of Beddington Church" (the Grenestrete could be identified with present-day Sandy Lane, and also suggests the presence of a village green). William received forty silver shillings for them and another piece of land, and Walter's annual rent for his new properties came to eight pence (four pence at Easter and four pence at the feast of St. Michael). Galfridus de Wodecot, Simon his son, and Thomas, son of Alured de Wodecot, were among the witnesses who signed this document.[23]

Galdricus le Hole de Wodecot gave his land in Beddington to his daughter, Agnes, on her marriage, and it became her own property when he died. She sold it in 1316 to the parson of Croydon's church, Lord John Maunsel, and others. Simon de Wodecot was one of the witnesses to the document, which was signed and sealed at Croydon.[23]

Simon de Wodecot had been one of the jurors in charge of assessments and collection of taxes in 1290 for the Wallington Hundred. Afterwards, these men also agreed to fines imposed on certain taxpayers "for concealment and other transgressions". Paradoxically, his name also appeared on the list of transgressors, and his fine amounted to seventeen shillings and four pence![20]

The last available full lists of taxpayers in Surrey were made in 1332 (those for 1334 have been lost). Taxation was based on the value of a person's moveable goods and, basically, represented one fifteenth of such wealth in the counties, and a tenth of the same in the boroughs. The following is a list of Woodcote's inhabitants in 1332 and shows their tax assessments (one fifteenth):-

De Rogero ate Grene	3s: 7d.	De Waltero ate Gren	2s: 6d.
De Willelmo de Charlewode	3s: 6d.	De Baldr' Frag'	2s: 0d.
De Ferand' de Spaigne	5s: 9d.	De Dragone ate holzeit'	16d.
De Ada Pik'	2s: 6d.	De Roberto Chekemete	8d.
De Thoma le Bole	12d.	De Johanne le Forester	3s: 6d.
De Willelmo Snel	3s: 6d.	De Relicta Crakeford	8d.
De Roberto Baudry	8d.	De Willelmo le Bole	8d.
De Johanne Brendwode	12d.		

The total tax for the village came to thirty-three shillings after some alterations.[20]

The Surrey Taxation Returns for 1332 showed that Woodcote had the same number of inhabitants as Beddington, where fifteen people paid a total of thirty-four shillings and three pence tax. Twelve taxpayers in Wallington had to pay the sum of twenty-four shillings and four pence, and thirty-one persons in the largest village, Bandon, made payments totalling fifty-six shillings and two pence.[20]

The corrupt practices of some of the collectors resulted in many complaints; therefore, after consultation with the taxpayers, a new method of collection was devised for 1334. Provided that the King did not receive less than the previous levy, no fresh assessments were made, except where general agreement was not obtained. Subsequent returns only showed the total amounts received from each village, and these sums remained unchanged except for slight, agreed variations. For example, Woodcote's tax rose to the sum of thirty-four shillings and six pence three farthings in 1336 and, thereafter, this figure was the assessment.

Over the next one hundred years, deductions were made for the relief of people burdened by extra levies raised to finance the country's various wars, and, in 1436, Woodcote received two reductions, one of six shillings and eight pence, and another of ten shillings. Also, a reduction of six shillings and eight pence was granted in 1545, and, afterwards, the sum required from the villagers remained at the fixed amount of twenty-seven shillings and ten pence three farthings, until payments ceased by the eighteenth century.[20]

From such evidence in the Surrey Taxation Returns, it seems logical to conclude that the ruins seen at Woodcote by Camden, Talbot, Symmes, Gale *et al.* in the sixteenth and seventeenth centuries, were not the villagers' homes. Woodcote's inhabitants had departed by 1736, when Salmon published his history of Surrey in which he described an old building here called a Chapel, which had been converted into a barn.[10]

In 1332, two members of the Forester family lived in the area – John in Woodcote and Roger in Bandon.[20] Within a few years, they were joined by William Forester, who purchased a croft, sixteen acres of land, and a grove[24] (perhaps the first farm at Woodcote Grove), and by Reginald Forester, when he acquired a small estate with lands in Beddington and Bandon, as well as a house, and paid eight shillings and four pence annually for them. In 1340, Edward III permitted him to hold them free of services by patent (a grant from the Crown). He became Sheriff of Surrey in 1334, and took his seat in Parliament as a Member for the county in 1348.[11]

Reginald Forester continued to enlarge his estate, and bought more properties in Beddington, Carshalton, Croydon and Woodmansterne. He purchased part of Woodcote from John of Waleton and John Bordwode (who can be identified with the John Brendwode in the Taxation Return of 1332), and leased some land there from Sir Thomas

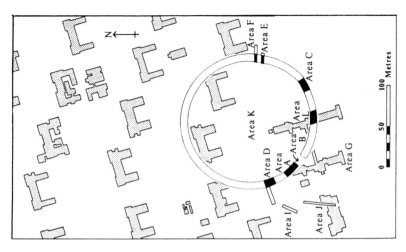

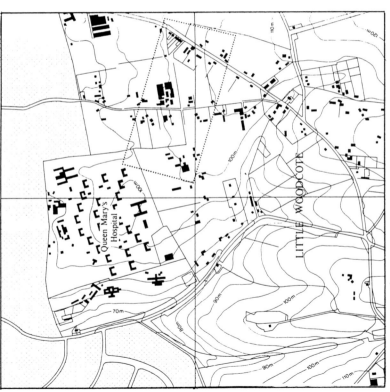

4 (*left*): The site location of worked flints found in Little Woodcote. 5 (*right*): Location and site plan of the late Bronze Age enclosure at the southern end of Queen Mary's Hospital grounds.

Huscarl,[24] who held one of Beddington's manors (later known as Beddington-Huscarls) which had been in his family's possession since King John's reign.[11]

Simon Roce, a Citizen Skinner of London, also owned part of Woodcote at this time.[15] He appeared in the Surrey Taxation Returns for 1332 as the richest man in Beddington, and paid ten shillings tax, which was three shillings and four pence more than Sir Thomas Huscarl had to pay.[20] Roce's estate included land in Bandon and Wallington.[15] Meanwhile, Simon de Wodecot became one of Sir Thomas's tenants, and held a toft (homestead) and six acres in the Beddington-Huscarl manor for the yearly service of one rose to the value of three shillings.[11]

Sir Thomas Huscarl was indirectly responsible for the changes of land ownership in Woodcote over the next one hundred years. The Carews of Moulsford were neighbours of his estates in Berkshire and, in 1333, he appointed Master William Carew as Chaplain of the Free Portion of Beddington.[6] William was the third son of Sir Nicholas, "Barron Carreu of Moulsford"[25] and, shortly after he took up his appointment as Portioner, two more members of his family, Nicholas and Reymond, became involved with property deals in Beddington and Surrey.[11, 27] Reymond's involvement was very short compared with that of Nicholas, who remained here throughout his life – and his descendants stayed for a further five centuries. They became the owners of all of Woodcote, including the Lodge there, which they held until the middle of the eighteenth century.

CHAPTER 3

THE EARLY CAREWS AND WOODCOTE

While Woodcote's villagers led a peaceful, rural life in the next two centuries, the Carews at Beddington were occupied with the acquisition of properties and wealth. The first Nicholas here was Master William's nephew and the eldest son of Thomas Carew[28] but Reymond's relationship to them has not yet been established. He is mentioned in two of the Carew Manuscripts in connection with the transfer of some lands in Beddington, Surrey – and elsewhere – in 1350 and 1369,[27, 29] and in the Calendars of the Close Rolls of Edward III's reign (45 Edward III).[30]

Nicholas held some property in Surrey by 1340, when Sir Thomas Huscarl and his wife, Lucy, "levied a fine to Master William de Carreu (portioner of the Church of Bedyngton) and Nicholas de Carreu of the Manor of Bedyngton, and 100 acres of wood and 20s. rent in Horlee, and the Advowson of the free portion of the church of Bedyngton...".[11] All three Carews survived the Black Death in 1349; and, in 1350, Reymond, Regnold Sheffield, and John At Thorne, gave Nicholas by "Dede credibill" their properties in Beddington and the manors of Bandon and Norbury, of which they were seized in fee (a freehold estate of inheritance) and, on his death, these passed to his son, another Nicholas, and his lawful heirs.[27] Afterwards, Reymond's involvement with lands here concerned only those granted to him, Regnold, and John, by Sir Thomas Huscarl, and included Sir Thomas's manor of Beddington, with the advowson of part of the Church, as well as property in Surrey, Berkshire and Oxfordshire, for which they paid the customary rents and services.[29]

Master William and Nicholas leased Home-Beddington from Lucy Huscarl's parents, Lord and Lady Willoughby, in 1352. Two years later, in 1354, Master William's death occurred[30] and he left his nephew to acquire that manor in 1359, as Home-Beddington's tenant-in-chief.[31] Sir Thomas Huscarl died about this time,[32] and his widow, Lucy, soon became Nicholas's wife. On 30th August, 1369, Reymond Carew, Regnold Sheffield, and John At Thorne, granted him and his heirs all of their properties they had leased from Sir Thomas, with the remainder to Sir Thomas's heirs.[29] Then the co-heirs to the Huscarl estates gave him releases from their respective claims and rights to these,[11] and he owned all of the Huscarls' lands in Woodcote, Surrey, Berkshire and Oxfordshire.

Meanwhile, Nicholas was Knight of the Shire of Surrey in 1362, and had served one year as the county's Member of Parliament.[11] Since 1358, he had been in the King's service, and his friendship with the famous prince, John of Gaunt,[33] helped with his advancement at court. He was Keeper of the Privy Seal from 1364 until 1376, and became the King's esquire in 1371.[26, 32] On 16th April, 1375, Edward III granted him and his heirs the free-warren of his lands in Croydon, Beddington, Carshalton, Mitcham, and Woodmansterne, and at "Purle and Mullesford" in Berkshire.[34] Also the King appointed him as one of the executors of his will, and he carried out this duty in 1377.[11]

After Edward III's death, Nicholas was among the seven persons appointed on 13th December, 1377, to make a truthful inventory of all jewels and other goods which disappeared when the King became prematurely senile two years before he died. The people involved in this duty had to give such items in their possession to the Keeper of the King's Wardrobe, Alan Stokes, and were recommended to disclose the names of others who had taken jewellery or articles from the royal household at that time. The penalty for failure to comply with these instructions meant forfeiture of all that could be forfeited from their own properties! Nicholas's part in the survey was probably successful, because, on 23rd February, 1379, he was committed to the keeping of young Richard II's leets of Beddington and Purley, with fines and profits from them, for a term of five years. However, he had to pay forty-three shillings and ninepence for these, in two equal portions at Easter and Michaelmas.[35]

After he had spent over fifty years in Beddington, Nicholas died on 17th August, 1390. Throughout his life, he retained his wealth by his ownership of property, and his large estates in Berkshire, Kent and Surrey passed to his son and heir, Nicholas,[35] who had ambitions to obtain more lands. He bought the properties in Beddington, Bandon, Croydon, Norbury and Woodcote owned at one time by Reginald Forester. One of the Carew manuscripts refers specifically to this part of his estate, and indicates that there was at this time a house of some substance in Woodcote, and called by the same name. This stood to the south of fourteen acres of land which a man called Renn or Renns had

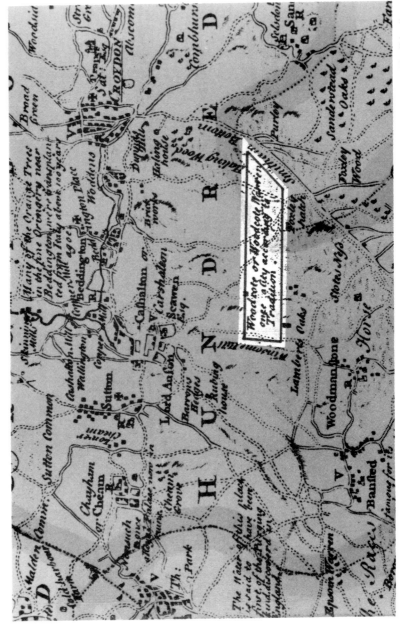

6 A section of Bowen's map of Surrey in 1755, showing "Woodcote, or Woodcote Warren, once a City according to Tradition".

purchased from Reginald Forester, and which was then bought by the second Nicholas[24]. It may be that this house was the 'Old Lodge' which, later, gave its name to the land in and around the present-day Woodcote Green, because the house was called a "Lodge" during the Carew's ownership of it. There is no proof that a building stood on Woodcote Hall's site before the early sixteenth century.[36]

We cannot know who occupied the principal house in medieval "Wodcott". Perhaps the richest man in the village in 1332, Ferand' de Spaigne,[20] lived here during the early fourteenth century, followed by Reginald Forester, when he owned the fourteen-acre field adjacent to it,[24] and subsequently by Renn.

Throughout his life, Nicholas continued to add to his estates, and received properties as rewards for services to both Richard II and Henry IV. He was Sheriff of Surrey and Sussex in October, 1400, and the Escheator of both counties in November 1403.[37] Woodcote's taxpayers probably suffered when, as Surrey's Sheriff again in 1405, he collected money from the county's richest people on the Treasurer of War's behalf to provide funds for the conquest of Welsh rebels, and relief of sieges at castles in the Duchy of Aquitaine, because Henry IV's own money had been spent to meet the "unwanted pressure of divers wars", and he could not pay the wages of the men-at-arms and the archers![37] After the King's death on 20th March, 1413, his son, Henry V, began more hostilities with France so that his purse soon emptied, and resulted in Nicholas's appointment on 27th March, 1420, to collected another tax levy to "preserve the royal rights and the safe-keeping of the realm"![38]

Two marriages provided Nicholas with eighteen children – three from his first wife, Isabella, and fifteen from the second, Mercy. Nearly all of them were dead when his own death occurred on 4th September, 1432. His eldest son, Thomas, had died two years before him; therefore his estates, including his lands in Woodcote, passed to another Nicholas, who was one of Mercy's two surviving children.[26]

The third Nicholas became the Escheator of Surrey and Sussex on 16th October, 1432, was a Member of Parliament for one year in 1439, and held the office of Surrey's Sheriff three times.[26] The county was in a bad state after the heavy taxation imposed to support Henry V's wars, but when hostilities with France ceased, and not all of the money had been spent, a decision was made to help the taxpayers. As a result, Woodcote's inhabitants received their two tax reductions for 1436,[20] and, perhaps, some further benefits when Nicholas Carew and William Sydney the Younger were given sixty-one pounds, twelve shillings and sevenpence farthing, and thirty pounds, sixteen shillings and three and five-eights pence, for distribution throughout the county as "part relief for poor towns, cities and boroughs that are desolate, laid waste or destroyed, over-impoverished or over-charged" by taxes levied earlier for the "defence of the realm".[39]

Nicholas and his wife, Margaret, had two sons, Nicholas and James, and three daughters. During a short period of uneasy peace in the Wars of the Roses, he died, in his early fifties, in April, 1458, and his estates passed to his eldest son. The fourth Nicholas was in Henry VI's service, but hostilities broke out again in 1459. After the King's defeat at the end of the following year, Edward IV was proclaimed King on 3rd March, 1461, and Nicholas's arrest followed a few days later.[26] Perhaps he convinced the Yorkists that he had changed sides, because he was free in November, and, by that time, had conspired with twenty-four other men wrongfully to accuse a Richard att Welle of Leatherhead of stealing four horses from the manor house at Beddington, and caused him to be arrested and detained in the Marshalsea prison. Probably as a result of this strange conspiracy, or because he had to prove his allegiance to the King, he was not given licence to enter freely into all of his estates in England until 29th January, 1466.[40]

Meanwhile, in 1459, in Woodcote's more peaceful, rural life, "Richard Compeworth of Whatyndon" rented from "Water Senys", a squire, the "game of conies and rabbits" on lands there and in Beddington, Bandon, Carshalton, Wallington, "Whatyngdon and Mesden", as well as a "loge called the gatehouse in Wodecote". Nicholas Carew also leased the same type of game for thirteen years commencing in 1465 from "John Elyngbrigg, squire, and William Bonyngton, gentleman", in their parts of Woodcote, Beddington and Carshalton, and paid thirteen shillings and four pence for the first year. The costs differed for the remainder of the lease after Nicholas's death[41] at the beginning of August, 1466, when he was thirty years old, and his only son, another Nicholas, was a minor aged three.[26]

The Escheators of Surrey and Sussex, Hugh Fenne and William Essex, held young Nicholas's estates from 15th August, 1466, until he came of age, during which time he became a Royal Ward.[42] After attaining his majority he caused problems for his family by dying, early in October, 1485, before he could marry and produce an heir. His local properties were given to Surrey's Escheator on 17th October, 1485,[43] until a decision was reached about the person entitled to inherit them.

A lengthy period of legal arguments began when Nicholas's three sisters claimed their brother's manors of Beddington, Bandon and Norbury, which, they hoped, would be divided between them. The eldest girl, Sanctia, had married Sir John Iwardby; Ann was then unmarried, and Elizabeth was the wife of Sir John's son, Edward Iwardby.[44] Obviously the Iwardbys hoped to gain some of the Carews' estates through their wives!

Livery of lands and licence to enter them without inquisition by writs of any kind was granted to the Iwardbys, their wives and Ann Carew on 6th December, 1485, because the girls were considered then as the heirs of the late young Nicholas.[44] However, the sisters only received the manor of Nutfield in Surrey to divide between them when, according to their father's will, their uncle James inherited his nephew's properties as young Nicholas's male heir,[45] and the arguments continued for about another seven years.

James Carew seems to have preferred to live on his own estate in Sussex and not at the manor house in Beddington during his short period of ownership of it,[26] probably because of the continuing dispute with the Iwardbys. He and his wife, Eleanor, had one son, Richard, who was aged "twenty-three or more" when James's death occurred on 22nd December, 1492. His properties went to the Escheators of Surrey, Sussex, Kent, Hertford and Bedford, but Surrey's Escheator held an Inquisition in February, 1493, to settle finally the Iwardbys' claim, and Richard's right to inherit all of the estates in that county.[43, 46]

Sir John Iwardby was far from satisfied with the small amount of property given to his wife and her sisters after their brother's death, and decided to challenge Richard's right to inherit the manors of Beddington, Bandon and Norbury. He stated that the freehold lands held by Reymond Carew, Regnold Sheffield and John At Thorne had previously belonged to Sir Thomas Huscarl and John of Bandon, and were given to the first Nicholas to pass on to his son, Nicholas, and his lawful heirs. His claim was now on behalf of himself and Sanctia (see Appendix II)[27] because Ann had married Christopher Trapnell and Elizabeth was Mrs. Walter Twynihoo.[11]

At the Inquisition, the most important parts of the evidence presented on Richard's behalf in answer to Sir John's claim proved that the lands in dispute never belonged either to Sir Thomas Huscarl, or John of Bandon, because the second Nicholas at Beddington purchased all of these from Reginald Forester, who, previously, had obtained them from a number of different local people (see Appendix II). Also, after the first Nicholas's death, the manors in question were held by "John Martyn,

7 Extracts from two of the Carew Manuscripts. (*above*): Refers to 'Woodcott' and a warren of conies called the 'Old Lodge' in 1520 (see Appendix III, question 4, for transcription). (*below*): Refers to acquisition of lands by Reginald Forester between 1390 and 1432 (see Appendix II(b), for transcription).

Roger Herron, John Gaynsford, John Corrf, William Selwian, William Bradford, Richard Fitzherbert and John Hall" to the second Nicholas's use, his heirs and his will, and, in accordance with that document, the properties passed to the third Nicholas and the heirs *male* of his body. Thus, when the fifth Nicholas died without issue, his nearest male heir was his uncle James, who was legally entitled to leave all of his estates to his only son.[43]

On 11th February, 1493, an order was given to the Escheator of Surrey in which it was stated that "the manor of Bedyngton is held of the King in chief by knight's service, and the rest of the manors of others than the King. That the said Richard Carue is of full age; to take fealty of said Richard and cause him to have full seisin of said manors, if they are in the King's hands by the death of said James, and for no other cause, as the King, for half a mark in the hanaper [the old office of the Court of Chancery] has respited his homage until March next."[43]

CHAPTER 4

ROYAL MATTERS AND RURAL AFFAIRS

After Richard and his family moved to Beddington, he was given several yearly appointments as Commissioner of the Peace for Surrey from 24th May, 1494, 1497 to 1501, and 1502 until May, 1506, during which time he became Sheriff of the county in 1501.[44] He was involved with affairs at the royal court, where his only son, Nicholas, was a great friend and favourite of young Prince Henry. Richard's knighthood, received on the battlefield at Blackheath in June 1497, was a reward for his service in Henry VII's army, hastily assembled to confront Audley's Cornish rebels, who gathered there at the end of their long protest march against high taxation.[26, 47]

By now, both the manor house at Beddington and "Wodcott" had probably fallen into disrepair. Since the death of the fourth Nicholas in 1466, these had been mostly in the Escheator of Surrey's hands, and it was unlikely that James Carew had any interest in them because of the dispute with the Iwardbys. Therefore, Sir Richard commenced major rebuilding work on his home around 1500,[26] and, at about the same time, a new lodge was built on the site of Woodcote Hall, while the old one was demolished and gave its name to the surrounding land which became a "warren of conyes" before 1520.[48]

The exact shape and size of the new "Woodcott" cannot be assessed, because it is hidden beneath, and incorporated in, the many later additions to it. Traces of the oldest walls can be seen, and are approximately two feet thick.[36] It had its own sheepwalk, which came down from southern Woodcote across the road to Wallington (now Woodcote Road) on to a twenty-acre field on the north side of the land called "the Old Lodge".[48] Possibly, some farm buildings were situated on the west side of the house, traces of which remain in part of the brickwork of the walled garden.[49]

"Woodcott's" owner received more properties as rewards for services to Henry VII, and, after the King's death on 22nd April, 1509, Sir Richard spent a good deal of time in France on young Henry VIII's behalf. Nicholas Carew was one of the King's constant companions, taking part in jousts, tournaments, masques and hunting with him, while the royal Great Wardrobe supplied some of his clothing. Nicholas's marriage to Elizabeth, a daughter of Queen Catherine's Vice-Chamberlain, Sir Thomas Bryan, met with Henry's approval. He attended the ceremony in December, 1514, at which six shillings and eight pence offering was paid for him by Lord Mountjoy.[50] In 1515, Sir Richard's daughter, Margaret, married John St. John, and it has been conjectured that the bridegroom received the Carew lands in Carshalton from his father-in-law on that occasion.[11]

During the year following his marriage, Nicholas was appointed Lieutenant of the Castle at Calais, and he joined his father there. In addition to his post of "squire of the Body", he became one of the King's cipherers with an annuity of fifty marks. On 3rd May, 1516, the Barons of the Exchequer were ordered to give him and his wife some properties in Wallington, Carshalton, Beddington, Woodmansterne, Woodcote and Mitcham, "acquired of Sir Laurence Ayhuer, Juliana, his wife, and Thomas, his son, to the value of forty marks in part payment of fifty marks as a marriage settlement". Confirmation of the 'Indented Deed' of 11th July, 1516, showed that they had the lease of "10 messuages and gardens, a pigeon house, 1,290 acres of land and 5s. rent". Before the end of that year, both he and his brother-in-law, Francis Bryan, were knighted.[50]

Although Sir Nicholas received more properties in Greenwich from the King in December 1517, within a few weeks both he and his wife had been banished from the royal court. Whatever the cause of the rift, it was soon healed, and, when the Archdeacon of Dorset, Richard Pace, wrote to Cardinal Wolsey on 27th March, 1518, he mentioned that: "Mr. Carew and his wife be re[turned] to the King's grace, too soon after mine [opinion]. [Me]Thinks they come by commandment."[50]

Both Sir Richard and his son were Commissioners of the Peace for Surrey in 1518, also Sir Nicholas became Sheriff of that county and of Sussex. Early in February, 1519, the King visited the manor house at Beddington "and stayed there a se'ennight". However, not long after the royal visit, Sir Nicholas went to France with Sir Francis Bryan and others, and caused Henry VIII to banish them all from his court for daring to compare it unfavourably with that of Francis I.[26]

Although Sir Nicholas was punished for his indiscretion by his appointment as Lieutenant of the lonely tower of Rysbank at the entrance to Calais harbour on 20th May, 1519, he was soon forgiven, and both he and his father were chosen to attend Henry VIII on his visit to

8 A preliminary drawing by Hans Holbein for his portrait of Sir Nicholas Carew, K.G., who owned 'Woodcott' from 1520 to 1539. He was the most illustrious of his family to own the house.

the famous Field of the Cloth of Gold to meet the French King.[26] "Mistress Carewe" was one of the gentlewomen who would accompany the Queen on that occasion.[50] Unfortunately, Sir Richard's death occurred in May, 1520, before the royal party set out for France.[26] His tomb is the earliest to be found in the Carew Chapel in Beddington Church.

Sir Nicholas inherited his father's estates, including the lands at Woodcote; "Woodcott"; and the rabbit warren called "the Old Lodge".[48] He spent most of his time at court, except for a visit to France in 1521, when he took presents to Francis I. In the same year, he acted as one of the jurors at the trial of Henry Stafford, Duke of Buckingham, who was found guilty of treason and executed.[26] Buckingham's estates were divided amongst the King's favourites, and Sir Nicholas's reward was the manor of Bletchingly in Surrey, as well as the stewardship of the manors of Brasted in Kent.[50] By the end of 1521, he had been appointed as Master of the King's Horse.[51]

As well as his appointments as Commissioner for the Peace in Surrey in 1522, 1524-6, 1528, and 1538, Sir Nicholas became Sheriff of Surrey and Sussex in 1528, and was Surrey's Member of Parliament in 1529.[11, 26] He was made Constable of Warwick Castle and town in July, 1528, and both he, and his brother-in-law, Sir Francis Bryan, were now entitled to "lodging in the King or Queen's lodging" when they accompanied them on their journeys.[51]

Despite the turbulent affair of the King's divorce, Sir Nicholas remained in the King's favour. His only son and heir, Francis, was born in 1530, and another royal visit to Beddington took place in July, 1531, when, allegedly, Anne Boleyn went there with the King.[26] Although conservative in matters of religion, he retained his loyalty to Henry VIII when the King broke all ties with Rome and declared himself head of the Church of England. The rewards for Sir Nicholas's allegiance were manors in Banstead and Walton-on-the-Hill; "the park, villeins, etc., in Charlwood and Horley in Surrey, with knight's fees, advowsons, etc., at an annual rent of 40 l."; and free warren "in all desmesne lands" (part of Queen Catherine's dowry on her marriage to Henry VIII). After the dissolution of the monasteries, he received more manors in Ebbesham (Epsom), Coulsdon and Horley, with advowsons of the churches, rectories, glebes and tithes belonging to them, and including those in Sutton "and elsewhere".[51]

In June, 1536, Sir Nicholas was involved in the unpleasant task of persuading young Princess Mary to accept her father as Supreme Head of the Church of England. As a result of his pleas to save herself from the threat of her own death on the scaffold, she repudiated the Pope's authority and acknowledged that the King's marriage to her mother, Queen Catherine, was unlawful and incestuous because she had been his brother's widow.[51]

Meanwhile, in Woodcote's rural peace, Sir Nicholas leased "Woodcott's" sheepwalk to Henry Burton of Carshalton,[48] who became the owner of "Mascalls" and its park (Carshalton Park) a few years later.[21] Burton also held the fourteen-acre field and had his own sheepwalk in Woodcote.[48] He attempted to gain a "free chapel and a little close of ground" in Wallington, which Henry VIII had given to Lady Carew. The subsequent argument ended in a law-suit, and a complaint was made to the King on Lady Carew's behalf. Sir Thomas Cromwell wrote to Henry Burton on 19th February, 1535, and informed him that these were the King's freehold properties, which must be restored to Lady Carew. He was ordered to cease legal proceedings to enable learned counsel to examine the matter.[51]

Henry VIII visited Sir Nicholas's home in Beddington again in 1538. The Lord Butler of England, John Hussey, wrote to the Vice-Admiral of the Fleet, Lord Lisle, on 9th April, 1538, and informed him: "the King is at the Master of the Horses and comes to Greenwich on Friday". After the royal party's departure, the livestock and food at the manor house needed replenishment, and Merton Priory's rich farmlands were among the local sources of supply. On 16th April, Richard Layton, priest to Sir Thomas Cromwell, wrote to him: "Here at Marten Abbey are eighteen fat oxen, whereof Sir Nicholas Carew desires part, forty fat sheep, 200 grs. of malt and 30 l. in ling and haberdyne. If I shall reserve any of these for your household, please certify me by Mr. Belasys, Marten Abbey, Tuesday morning".[51] (Ling was a food fish and haberdyne a dried, salted cod.)

Towards the end of 1538, Sir Nicholas's life was in jeopardy after the arrest of Lord Montacute, Sir Edward Neville, and the Marquis of Exeter, who was the King's cousin, on suspicion of plotting to overthrow the government, and place Reginald Pole (later a Cardinal) on England's throne. Their relatives and others involved in the plot were also imprisoned. Sir Nicholas had been closely associated with Exeter through his duties in the Privy Chamber,[11, 26] and the King, possibly prompted by Cromwell, now waited for an opportunity to accuse his friend of treason and obtain his manor house with its vast parklands, as well as his large estates!

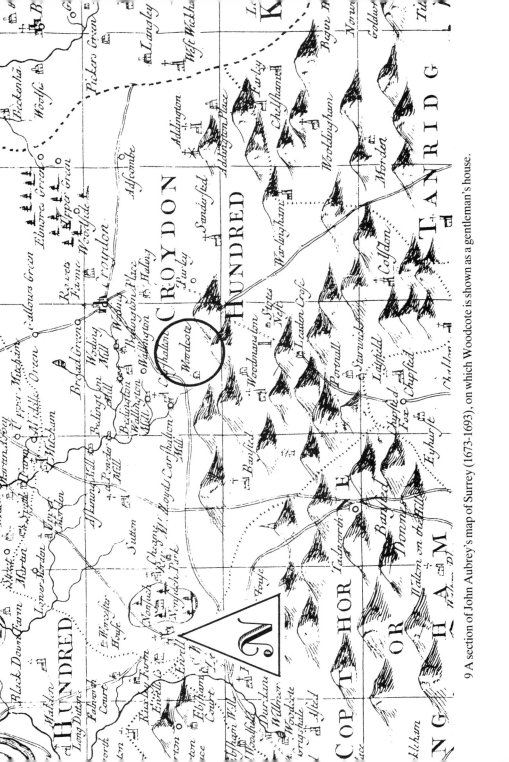

9 A section of John Aubrey's map of Surrey (1673-1693), on which Woodcote is shown as a gentleman's house.

Finally, Sir Nicholas foolishly argued with the King during a game of bowls, and Henry took advantage of this situation by ordering his arrest. The Carew estates were confiscated immediately afterwards, and Sir Michael Stanhope was appointed as "Keeper of the Manor House at Beddington".[11, 26] After Sir Nicholas's trial, at which he was found guilty of treason, he was beheaded on 3rd March, 1539. Elizabeth, his widow, took refuge in a house at Wallington (perhaps this was "Woodcott") with her four daughters and one son, Francis,[26] who was nine years old. On 11th March, 1539, she wrote to Sir Thomas Cromwell and appealed to him to act as mediator on behalf of herself and the children, and ask for the King's permission to continue to hold Wallington and Bletchingly which he had previously granted to her. Also, because of her husband's execution, she could not claim her dower, and requested some of his properties in Sussex, so that, altogether, she could receive an annual income of just over three hundred marks. However, she had to wait for an answer to her requests. Meanwhile, another royal journey began, and on 30th June, 1539, John Hussey informed Lord Lisle: "...the King moves this night unto Beddington, late the Master of the Horse place, then to Hampton Court, thence on 5th July towards Portsmouth, and so continues his progress..."[51]

In August, 1539, Lady Carew received some of her late husband's properties at Plumpton and Fletching in Sussex, the advowson of Plumpton's church, the house in Wallington where she lived, another one there "late in the tenure of the prior of St. Mary Overy in Southwark", and other houses, for the term of her life. After her death, these passed to her son, Francis, and his male heirs.[51] It seems likely that the King's grant also included "Woodcott".

Young Francis grew up with little hope of regaining his father's estates. He probably spent his boyhood with his mother, who lived in retirement at Wallington until her death in about 1546, when he inherited the properties granted to her by the King.[26] By then, the manor of Beddington and some of the lands in Woodcote had been given to a Walter Gorge.[11]

After Henry VIII's death in 1547, young Edward VI decided to exchange his late father's properties in Beddington and Woodcote for some manors in Essex which he had bestowed upon his Lord Chamberlain, Thomas, Lord Darcy. Thus Lord Darcy received: "the Manor, Mansion and Park of Bedington...and copses within the Warren of Woodcote in a close called 'The Old Lodge', and a wood on the west part of the Lodge of Francis Carew...and a rabbit warren in Woodcote,

10 (*opposite, above*): The house in the park at Carshalton which was Sir William Scawen's home. Drawn and engraved by J. Hassell. (*below*): The front elevation of the mansion designed by Leoni for Thomas Scawen. It was intended to replace the house shown above.

Bedington, late in the tenure of Sir Michael Stanhope...", as well as other estates.[11]

One of Lord Darcy's relatives, Sir Arthur Darcy, supervised the local estates, including those at Woodcote. In 1550 he issued an order to his bailiff, Thomas Mabson, to carry out some work on the Lodge at Woodcote. Mr. Mabson's accounts of "rents for the half year to Annunciation, 4 Edward VI" for repairs on Woodcote Lodge and the mansion house at Wallington showed that the carriage of a "windfall logge from Woodcott (unto) Walyngton" cost sixpence; and two sawyers for sawing the same log into joists for the Lodge came to three shillings and sixpence.[52] Mr. Mabson also paid two shillings and one penny for five hundred nails, and two shillings and two pence for a lock, hooks and hinges. The carpenter, "John Smythe" received five shillings and three pence for his "Workmanship aboute the sayd lodge", and the bailiff's total payments for the work on the house amounted to thirteen shillings and sixpence.[53] However, the use of a "windfall logge" does suggest that the wood for the joists was not of the best quality! In the same year, eight pence was "payed for carryge of a lode of wood from Woodcott to Wallyngton for to nele the greate oven", and the rents included: "Item of Nycholas Collgatt for the game of conyes lying and being in Woodcott xl s."(40 s.)[53]

On 20th November, 1552, Thomas, Lord Darcy, leased a sheepgate and way in Woodcote, "Roke" in Coulsdon, together with warren, woods, underwoods and sheepwalks, to George Butler, a gentleman of Croydon, for a term of twenty-one years.[54] Meanwhile, Princess Mary had, perhaps, taken Francis Carew into her household at Kenninghall, and he was in her service after she became Queen in 1553. In the following year, she restored Beddington and his late father's former properties in Surrey to him, and to make sure that these remained in his possession, he took a new conveyance by purchase from Lord Darcy[11, 26] and retained Thomas Mabson as bailiff of his estates.[55]

On 22nd May, 1561, Francis made an agreement with George Butler to continue to have the use of the sheepgate and way in Woodcote, which he had held by virtue of the lease from Lord Darcy; and it was also agreed that he should have fifty of Francis's sheep on this land at the cost of their owner.[54] After Mr. Butler's lease had ended, the following entry was made in Mr. Mabson's accounts: "I aske alowance for thys yers rent of Woodcott which Mr. Butler pd to my m[r] [master] the sum of x li."(£10)[55] which suggests that he was the tenant of "Woodcott". In 1574, Francis's bailiff paid sixteen pence "to allin for groobbinge of to oks at

12 The famous Cheam School was moved into this building in 1719 by the headmaster, the Revd. Daniel Sanxay, who was Dr. Edmund Sanxay's father.

13 The pigeon house (demolished in 1902) belonging to the West Cheam manor
house.

Wodcott"[55] (i.e. to Alan, or Allen, for grubbing out two oaks at Woodcote).

The Burtons continued to lease "Woodcott's" sheepwalk after Henry's death in 1543. His eldest son, Nicholas, was also dead, and Nicholas's widow, Ellen, renewed the lease in 1561, for twenty-one years at an annual rent of twenty-six shillings and eight pence, and the "keeping of one hundred sheep" owned by Francis Carew and George Butler.[48] Mrs Burton had received "Mascalls" in Carshalton for life, before it passed to her oldest boy, Richard.[21]

By 1561, Francis's cousin, John St. John, had inherited the western side of Woodcote in Carshalton from his father. The villagers were allowed to put their cattle, sheep and horses on the pasture here at certain times of the year, but a Mr. Fromans (or Furmans) decided to rebel against this rule and graze his sheep there at the wrong time. The manorial court was informed on 22nd May, 1561, that he had occupied Pillory Down. On 24th October, 1561, it was reported that he had "cut heath and kept sheep" there, and "process" was ordered against him for trespass. He continued to use the land until 6th October, 1567, when he was fined after refusing to let the bailiff of the manor "come on Pyllerydowne".[56]

Francis Carew had gained a reputation as a skilful gardener, and, probably, had learnt his horticultural expertise during his youth at Wallington, and at his Lodge in Woodcote, where the walled garden could be attributed to him because parts of the older brickwork date from about the mid-sixteenth century.[49] He re-designed his gardens at Beddington and became famous for his orange trees grown out in open ground. These were covered over in winter, when stoves provided heat to protect the trees from frosts.[14] The orangery wall, which still stands in the garden, is later than this time, but an earlier one may have given shelter from the cold northerly winds. He was one of the first gardening experts to achieve good crops of oranges by this method of cultivation.[11,14] It is possible that his trees came from France. Another keen gardener of that time, Sir William Cecil, the Secretary of State, wrote to his son, who was in Paris in 1562, and requested him to: "send over a lemon, a pomegranate and a myrtle tree, with directions for their culture, which may be brought to London with Mr. Carew's trees."[57]

As well as his interest in horticulture, Francis was involved in local affairs as a Justice of the Peace. The records for Kingston Assizes showed that he received his knighthood sometime between 8th March and 23rd July, 1576, because the entry for the latter date was the first to show him as Sir Francis Carew.[58]

14 An engraving of William Scawen and Jane Butterfield. It was used as the frontispiece for a book giving details of Miss Butterfields trial.

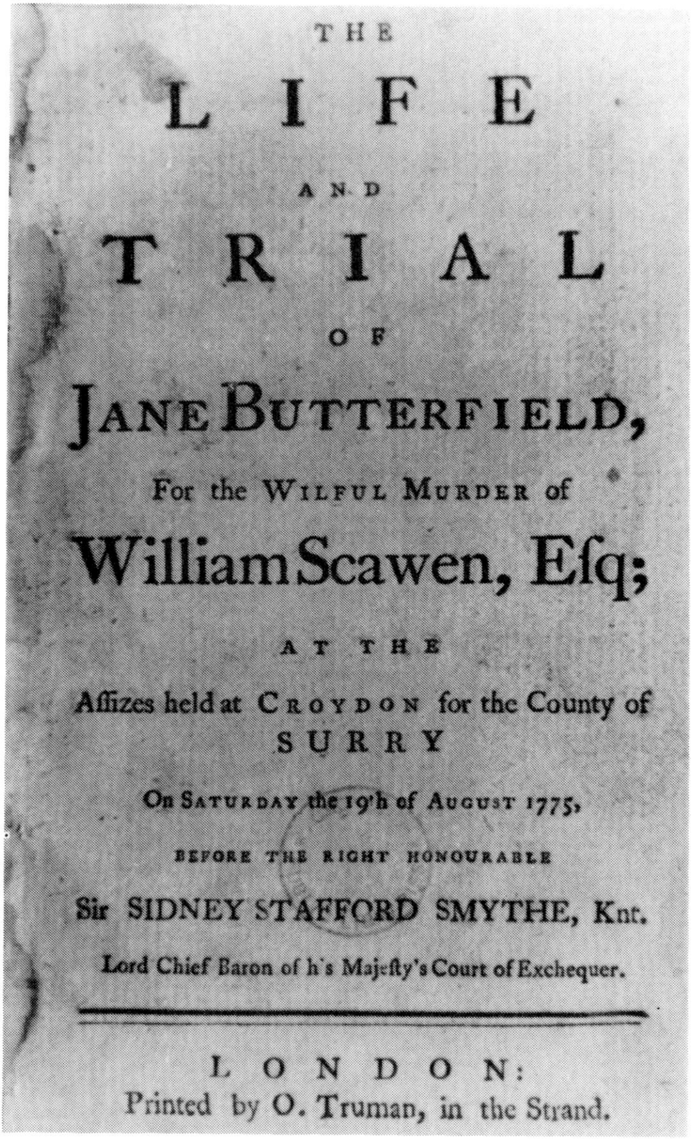

THE

LIFE

AND

TRIAL

OF

JANE BUTTERFIELD,

For the WILFUL MURDER of

William Scawen, Efq;

AT THE

Affizes held at CROYDON for the County of
SURRY

On SATURDAY the 19'h of AUGUST 1775,

BEFORE THE RIGHT HONOURABLE

Sir SIDNEY STAFFORD SMYTHE, Knt.

Lord Chief Baron of h's Majefty's Court of Exchequer.

LONDON:
Printed by O. Truman, in the Strand.

15 The title page of the same book.

According to Sir Francis's account book ending at Easter in 1584, he then received £48.11s.11d. for the half year's rent of farms in the manors of Beddington, Bandon and Woodcote.[59] The Burtons' lease of "Woodcott's" sheepwalk had ended in 1582, but they still retained one of their own in Woodcote and held lands there.[48] They were now important people in the local community. Ellen's son, Richard, received "Mascalls" and its park on his marriage to Anne Hampton in 1574. He inherited a lease on Crosslands, an estate probably in Beddington and Carshalton, obtained Chamberlains in Beddington, and bought John St. John's moiety of Carshalton in 1580. His youngest sister, Mabel, married the Duke of Norfolk's second son, Viscount Howard of Bindon, and established a connection with the royal court for her family.[21, 60]

Richard tried to claim a small piece of Sir Francis Carew's land by "Woodcott's" sheepwalk[48] shortly before his death on 12th October, 1590. After he had died, his estates were held in trust for ten years to enable his widow to provide for their four sons until they attained their majorities. His eldest son and heir, another Henry, was then twelve years old, and became a Royal Ward.[11, 21]

Anne Burton also thought that the half-acre of land by "Woodcott's" sheepwalk belonged to her eldest son's estate. Consequently, a dispute arose between her and its tenant, William Paire, who leased it from Sir Francis. Finally, the matter was settled in the Court of Wards, where Sir Francis's ownership of it, and Mr. Paire's tenancy, were both established.[48] (See Appendix III)

Some property in Wallington which had belonged to Sir Edward Dymock was transferred to Sir Francis by a James Harrington in 1596.[47] On 19th May in the same year, Elizabeth I wrote to the Bishop of Winchester requesting him to provide a suitable reward as a token of her appreciation of Sir Francis's long, loyal service to her. After lengthy deliberations, which lasted for about another year, the Bishop informed the Queen that he was ready to grant a benefit of £1,200.[57]

It is now known that Elizabeth I made several visits to Beddington. Her earliest visit there was on 4/5th August, 1559, when she was nearing the end of a three-week "progress" in Kent and Surrey (the first summer one of her reign) and she stopped at Sir Francis's home for a mid-day dinner on her way from Croydon to Nonsuch. In 1598, the Queen stayed with Sir Francis at Beddington during the second half of September (dates unknown)[61] and she visited him again in 1599 when he proved his horticultural expertise by covering his cherry tree with canvas to hold back the fruit from ripening, so that she could enjoy cherries on her visit.[11, 47]

According to an old local legend, Elizabeth I held a clandestine meeting with Sir Walter Raleigh (or Ralegh) at "Woodcott", and used the secret passage from Beddington's manor house to the Lodge at Woodcote for that purpose! The existence of the story could suggest that she stayed at Beddington when Raleigh was her favourite at court (between 1581 and 1588). However, it would be very difficult to define what connection, if any, Sir Walter had with the house at Woodcote.

The Queen's last visit to Beddington was on 14th August, 1600.[61] After her death in March 1603, Sir Francis carried on with the administration of his local estates during the first eight years of James I's reign. By then, William Black had replaced Thomas Mabson as Sir Francis's bailiff, and Mr. Black's accounts for 1606 show that the quit-rent for Beddington and Bandon was £1.9s.8d., while the farm-rent for the tenants there, at Woodcote and in the Park, came to a total of £107.8s.8d.[62]

Sir Francis died unmarried on 16th May, 1611, at the age of eighty-one years.[11] Most of his estates, including those at Woodcote, passed to his nephew, Nicholas Throckmorton, youngest son of Sir Francis's sister, Lady Anne, and he then took the surname and arms of Carew. He was in James I's service and received a knighthood in 1613, despite the fact that his sister, Bess, was married to Sir Walter Raleigh, whom the King had imprisoned on a charge of treason, for which he was finally executed in October, 1618.[26]

After James I's death, and during Charles I's conflict with Parliament, both Sir Nicholas and his son, Sir Francis, supported the King's cause. Sir Nicholas's age of eighty years prevented him from taking part in the fighting when the Civil War began. He died in 1644, and his estates passed to his grandson, another Nicholas, but were left for Sir Francis's use in young Nicholas's minority.[11, 26] Sir Francis survived his father by another five years, and in 1644 he was fined £2,000 to save his family's properties for "appearing to be in service against Parliament". The Commonwealth imposed heavy taxes on royalist landowners, and he found it necessary to mortgage some of the estate. The debts remained unpaid in future years, and the subsequent heirs inherited them.[26]

The other landowners in Woodcote, the Burton family, did not fare so well. Young Henry, who was a Royal Ward in Elizabeth I's reign, became a Knight of the Bath in 1603, and his son and heir, another Henry, was born on 1st November 1609, but only lived to the age of twenty-one years.[63] Although he prospered in James I's reign, and supported Charles I, Sir Henry, who was sixty-four years of age when the Civil War began, failed to change his allegiance to Cromwell at the end of the hostilities and resultant financial difficulties forced him to sell off some of his estate. He died in 1647, and was the last lord of Carshalton's manor to base his wealth on land ownership. His depleted properties passed to his brother, Charles, who sold them. Over the next fifty years, the lands on Woodcote's western side in Carshalton belonged to many absentee owners of the manor.[21]

Young Nicholas was fourteen years old when Sir Francis died in 1649. He was left in the care of Carew Raleigh, Sir Walter's youngest son, who received favourable treatment by the Commonwealth's supporters, due to their sympathies towards his late father, and disapproval of his execution by James I. Beddington's manor house was leased to the Earl of Warwick from 1649 to 1653, to assist with Nicholas's financial problems.[26] Possibly, Nicholas and his mother resided at "Woodcott" during this time. The Lodge was a house of some importance in the parish and, probably, was occupied by Mr. Raleigh, who, later, was credited with eight chimneys in the Surrey Hearth Tax return of 1664.[64] The west wing was added to it in the seventeenth century;[36] also two small, rectangular gatehouses[65] at the entrances to the little park around it – one by the Hollow Way (Woodcote Road) and another at the end of a driveway into the Bridle Way (Boundary Road). These additions took place either before the Civil War when the family's finances were more healthy, or in Carew Raleigh's tenancy.

After Charles II's restoration in May, 1660, Nicholas received his knighthood. He spent part of his time at Beddington's manor house and the Surrey Hearth Tax return for 1664 showed that he had fifty chimneys in the parish.[26, 64] He married Susannah, a daughter of Sir Justinian Incham (or Isham), another staunch royalist, who had suffered under the Commonwealth rule for not changing his allegiance. Nicholas's wife presented him with seven children: Francis, Susan, Justiniana, Jane, Phillipa, Nicholas and Richard. Phillipa's grandson was destined to inherit the family's estates later in the eighteenth century.[11, 26]

In 1671, Carshalton's villagers were allowed pasture for their sheep in the manor's common fields as far south as Parker's Close.[56] At that time, Woodcote Lodge stood on the edge of a great tract of downlands collectively known as Banstead Downs, which stretched from Croydon to Epsom, and from Reigate to Sutton.[66] The seventeenth century writer, Richard Blome, said that these downs "affordeth great delight for Hawking, Hunting and Horse-races". The latter sport commenced in

16 Cheam House. The home of Dr. Edmund Sanxay where William Scawen died on 8th July, 1775.

James I's reign and, except for the period of Commonwealth rule, racing began here daily at noon. Charles II and Samuel Pepys were among the distinguished visitors to the race-meetings.[67] Thus, "Woodcott" would have been a desirable residence for any sporting gentleman to acquire as a tenant.

Sir Nicholas's eldest son, Francis, married Anne Boteler in 1684,[26] and, as part of their marriage settlement, the bride received the manors of Norbury and Walton on the Hill, and farms in Banstead and Beddington, which she was to hold for life and then pass on to the male heirs of her marriage or, if none, then to her brother-in-law, Nicholas, in tail-male. When Sir Nicholas died in 1688, his estates were held in trust for his widow's use by Sir Justinian Incham, John Iwardby, Antony Boyen of Camberwell, Surrey, and John Spencer of Inner Temple, London, and after her death the lands and properties would pass to Sir Francis and his heirs.[68]

Between 1688 and 1690, Sir Francis, his brother, Richard, and sister, Jane, died, and the young heir to the Carew estates, another Nicholas, was about two years old. Little Nicholas's mother, Anne, also died in 1690, and left him and her daughter, Elizabeth, in Dame Susannah's care, although their Boteler grandfather claimed that he was the boy's rightful guardian. The dispute ended in law-suits, and care of the properties was divided between the grandparents, with an official receiver, Mr. Charles Byne of Carshalton, to supervise the management of them.[26]

Nicholas attained his majority in 1707 and married Elizabeth Hacket in the following year. Despite financial problems, he found enough money to carry out major alterations to Beddington's manor house. He was the first Beddington Carew to receive a baronetcy, which was given to him in August, 1714, shortly after George I's accession, and he became a Member of Parliament in the same year. He and his wife had four children, but only two survived: his heir, Nicholas Hacket, and Anne. He died suddenly in March 1726-7 (the New Year began in that month then) when he was about forty years old, and once again the estates passed to a minor.[26, 47]

Young Nicholas Hacket Carew was seven years old when his father died and his mother, Dame Elizabeth, became his guardian until he attained his majority, but she married a William Chetwynd in the meantime.[26] The financial problems of her son's estates, and the debts incurred by her brother-in-law, Walter Chetwynd, forced her to mortgage the manors of Horley, Burstow and Banstead, to obtain

£10,000. She repaid £6,000 out of the total loaned to her, and had paid off Walter's debts before her death in 1740, when Nicholas was aged twenty. Therefore, he inherited a debt of £4,000 and still owed his mother monies from his estate's income. She also left him her house in Dover Street, London, and all of her household goods, furniture, plate and jewels.[69] He was the last male heir in the direct line of his part of the family, because his marriage with Katherine Martin in 1741 produced two daughters: Catherine in 1742, and Elizabeth in 1745. Neither of the girls enjoyed good health, and Elizabeth's life ended in 1752.[11]

During the time in which he had complete control over his properties, Sir Nicholas did not solve his financial problems, and was obliged to sell some of his estates.[26] His father had sold a piece of land in Wallington to Edmund Byne in 1719, and Edward, the eleventh Earl of Derby, and the Earl's distant relative, Sir John Stanley, became owners of some of the Carew lands there before 1751.[70] By the end of 1746, Woodcote Lodge had a new owner when it was purchased by Mr. William Scawen.

CHAPTER 5

THE SCAWENS AND WOODCOTE

William was the youngest son of Sir Thomas and Dame Martha Scawen. Sir Thomas's brother, Sir William, was the first member of that family to own property in Woodcote after his arrival in Carshalton in 1696, when he bought Mascalls and its park and a moiety of the manor,[21, 71] with its lands on Woodcote's western side. Both brothers were wealthy merchants, and were two of the sons of Robert Scawen of Horton in Buckinghamshire.[11]

Sir William made his fortune by supporting William III's defence of the Netherlands against French invasion forces, and received a knighthood for his financial aid in 1695. He became the Governor of the new Bank of England founded in the previous year. His wife, Mary, died in 1700 at the age of thirty-three, and he erected a fine marble monument in her memory in Carshalton's church. He was elected to Parliament three times in Queen Anne's reign. He owned properties in England and Ireland, and added to those in Surrey throughout his life, including another moiety of Carshalton in 1713.[11, 47] In June, 1719, he leased the "Manor House" there with its grounds and eight acres called "Bullens Closes", for a term of sixty-one years, from Joseph Eyles, another wealthy London merchant.[73]

In about 1714, Sir William attempted to buy Carshalton House and its estate while acting as the Trustee appointed by the Commission of Bankrupt, who tried to settle the financial and legal affairs of the two previous owners, Edward Carleton and Dr. John Radcliffe. Sir William's offer was rejected, and one made by Sir John Fellowes was accepted[74] which, probably, caused feelings of bitter disappointment on the loser's part, and his jealousy increased when Sir John employed Charles Bridgeman to improve the grounds around his home in 1719-1721.[75] Sir William then had plans drawn up and a model constructed for a magnificent mansion to replace Mascalls, but died in October 1722 before he achieved his ambition to own the best and largest house in the village! His memorial was added to that of his wife in Carshalton Church.[21]

17 The Greyhound Inn at Carshalton. It was owned by John Durand from 1773 until 1778, and then by his son, John Hodsdon Durand, until 1819. Drawn and engraved by J. Hassell.

Because he had no children of his own to inherit his wealth and estates, Sir William left the bulk of his properties and his money to his nephew, Thomas, the eldest son of Sir Thomas. He gave legacies and annuities to his other nieces and nephews, but the largest sums went to his brother's family: Louis, Robert, William, Susannah and Martha, who each received £7,000.[72]

Thomas became Carshalton's lord of the manor, with its lands in western Woodcote, and inherited his uncle's properties in Buckinghamshire, Surrey, Yorkshire, Cornwall, Wiltshire, Berkshire, "and elsewhere in England, Great Britain and Ireland", when Sir William's will was proved on 2nd November 1722. He also received £10,000 with instructions to use it for the intended mansion to replace Mascalls as near as possible to the "Modell" made previously.[72]

Thomas's father, Sir Thomas, had become a Citizen and Freeman of the City of London by 1691, when he married Miss Martha Wessell. Under the terms of their marriage agreement, he was obliged to spend £6,000 to buy freehold properties within forty miles of the City to hold for life; and, on his death, these would provide for his wife and children, and satisfy Martha's rights of dower and those of a Freeman's widow.[76] He and Martha lived in Banstead[77] and their four sons and two daughters were born there. He received his knighthood in 1714, and became a Member of Parliament in the following year. Although he held the office of Alderman of Cornhill Ward, he never rose to the position of Sheriff and, thus, be eligible to become the Lord Mayor.[47, 78]

In 1723, Sir Thomas moved his wife and family to Carshalton, where he leased a house, together with other lands and premises, from Joseph Eyles. He bought "Piggs Farm" (later called Hill Farm) there, and some property in Cheam and Cuddington. Lastly, in the early part of 1730, he acquired more properties in Reigate, Headley and Walton on the Hill.[76]

Young William had left school by 1st December, 1726, when he commenced his seven years' apprenticeship with his father's former business partner, Mr. Samuel Swinfen, so that he could be "bred up a merchant".[76] Probably he was educated at Cheam School, judging by his life-long friendship with Edmund Sanxay, whose father, the Reverend Daniel Sanxay, became the School's headmaster in 1719.[79] Edmund chose a medical career and, later, was the Scawens' family surgeon.[80]

Sir Thomas died on 22nd September, 1730,[81] and left his leasehold house, lands and premises in Carshalton to his widow, Dame Martha, together with the contents of their other residences, including one in London, his "Coaches, Chariots and horses", and all jewellery belonging to both of them. She received £1,650 for herself, £200 for mourning, and two sums of £10 for distribution among the poor of Horton in Buckinghamshire, and Carshalton. She became entitled to all rents and profits from his properties in Reigate, Headley, Walton on the Hill, Buckland, Cheam and Cuddington, for life; but if either Robert or William tried to obtain this money they would be penalised by receipt of less of their father's real estate, so that equivalent amounts could be taken from their shares to compensate their mother![76]

Because Thomas had inherited Sir William's estates, and had been assured of inheriting Horton in Buckinghamshire, he would only be entitled to "Piggs Farm" and other lands in Carshalton after Dame Martha's death. Also when their mother died, Robert would receive the properties in Reigate, Headley and Walton on the Hill, and William those in Cheam and Cuddington, and the Colley House Farm in Reigate. Robert's share was to pass to his lawful heirs, or, if none, then to William, Louis and Thomas, while William's would go to Louis or Thomas if he had no lawful issue.[76]

Louis was given £6,000 on his marriage, but was to receive another £4,000. Susannah and Martha had already been "fully advanced" before their father died, and no further provisions were made for them in Sir Thomas's will. Only Robert and William remained "unadvanced", and were bequeathed one moiety of Sir Thomas's personal estate to be divided equally between them, while the other half was left in trust for Mr. Samuel Swinfen to invest on their behalf for their education, maintenance and advancement until they reached respectively the age of twenty-three, when they would receive their shares.[76]

Apparently, Sir Thomas had suspicions that William would refuse to complete his apprenticeship with Mr. Swinfen without some kind of encouragement. Therefore, if Dame Martha died during that time, the leasehold house in Carshalton would be held in trust by Thomas for the remainder of its lease, and if William completed his seven years as an apprentice, or as much of that period necessary to meet with Mr. Swinfen's or Thomas's approval, then he received this property – but failure on William's part meant that it passed to Robert![76]

By now, Thomas owned all of Carshalton's manor, having bought Stone Court in 1728. He lived at Mascalls until the latter part of his life, and he and his wife, Tryphena, had a son, James and three daughters. He gained a reputation as a spendthrift because of his extravagant improvements to his park, and the grandiose plans for a larger mansion there than envisaged by his uncle, for which he purchased expensive building materials.[11, 71, 82] Due to his interest and expertise in botany and horticulture, Richard Bradley, the author, naturalist and Professor of Botany at Cambridge, dedicated his *Dictionarium Botanicum* to him in 1728, which was the first work of its kind in England. In 1732, he was mentioned in *The Great Improvement of Commons that are enclosed*, and this, too, could have been Bradley's work.[83] Also, he represented Surrey in the House of Commons from 1727 until 1741.[84]

Although Thomas's magnificent mansion designed by Leoni never materialised, he spent more than his uncle's bequest of £10,000 on it, and, allegedly, the final sum came to £100,000![85] His financial resources were seriously depleted by the end of 1741, and he was forced to sell part of his valuable collection of paintings, including works by Watteau, Rembrandt, Van Dyck, Rubens, Michelangelo and Sir Peter Lely, as well as his bronzes, statues and other works of art. The sale of these items took place from 25th to 28th January, 1742, at Cock's Salerooms in London,[86] where another painting owned by him, *Liberality, and Modesty*, after Guido, was sold for £15.15s.0d. to Lord Burlington in 1744.[87]

Probably, William completed his apprenticeship with Samuel Swinfen. He had the advantage of beginning his career as a merchant with a considerable amount of money inherited from his father and uncle. However, he chose a different way of life from that of his brothers, and indulged in some of the riotous living and debauchery enjoyed by other Georgian gentlemen of his social status, but avoided any financial problems. Nevertheless, he gained a reputation, and when Barrett wrote about him in the more strict and sober late nineteenth century, he said: "...he seems to have been not only a notorious evil-liver but was devoted to quacks and quackery"![88]

William was the rated occupier of some property in Carshalton until October, 1746,[89] when, probably, he moved to "Woodcote" in Beddington's parish, although the exact date has not been traced. His parklands in front of the house were enlarged by his lease of two acres of land in Wallington from Edward Stanley, the eleventh Earl of Derby, and Nicholas Wood, on 25th October, 1751,[70] and he obtained more lands in Carshalton in 1760.[89] Also, he had a residence in London, where he rented rooms in Somerset House.[80] His mother, Dame Martha, left her leasehold premises in 1753, which were taken over by Lady Pomfret at the end of that year.[89]

Although William never married, he did have a daughter, Mary Fling, who was "commonly called Mary Scawen".[90] It seems unlikely that

18 The Little Woodcote Farmhouse (now Little Woodcote Cottages). It was designed by Robert Mylne and built in 1790-1791 for John Hodson Durand.

either Mary, or her mother, lived with him at Woodcote Lodge, but in 1763, he decided to have a female companion to share his home. He used a procuress's services and obtained a young girl of fourteen, Jane Butterfield, whom he seduced and then persuaded to live with him.[80, 88]

He paid for Jane's education, and treated her with such kindness that, eventually, she grew to love him. Also, he arranged that she would inherit his estate on his death. She became well known in the neighbourhood for her charity to the poor, and this was extended to Mrs Fling, who lived in poverty before her death and only received an annuity of five pounds from William. Consequently, Jane made an additional allowance of twenty pounds a year out of her own money.[186] William's sister, Martha, Lady Mead, had lived in Woodmansterne with her husband, Sir Nathaniel,[91] but after his death, she returned to Carshalton in 1765, and took over the Dower House in the High Street, which belonged to Thomas.[71] From events which occurred ten years later, it seems likely that Miss Butterfield's position at Woodcote met with her disapproval!

Dame Martha Scawen died at Reigate on 29th June, 1766,[11] and her sons then inherited their shares of Sir Thomas's estate. Thomas received the Carshalton properties, Robert had those in Reigate, Headley and Walton on the Hill, and William took over the Colley House Farm in Reigate, and the property in Cheam and Cuddington.[76] One of his houses at Cheam was "a Messuage or Mansion House...now or late called the School House...formerly in the occupation of Henry Day, Clerk, afterwards of Robert Lloyd, Gentleman..."[92] Therefore, it had been the first Cheam School, of which the Reverends George Aldrich, Henry Day and Robert Lloyd were the headmasters, before the establishment was transferred to new premises in 1719 by the Reverend Daniel Sanxay.[79]

It seems likely that William's School House was the West Cheam Manor House, because the name of "Manor House" appeared on Ordnance Survey maps for the later premises, which stood on the site of the Tabor Court flats before 1934. After the Reverend Mr. Day's death in 1701, the owners of the old school, John Adams and Samuel Pierson, advertised for another tenant, and described the building in the London Gazette for 31st March, 1701, thus: "A large House fit for a Gentleman, with a good orchard, Pidgeon-house and four acres of ground at Cheame near Epsom in Surrey, having been an eminent Boarding-School above sixty years, is to let, the Master being lately dead..."[79] The Manor House demolished in 1796 also had "a very fine brick pigeon house with an ogee lead roof...", and this was pulled down in 1902, when the houses in Park Road were built.[93]

The old indentures examined recently in respect of William's Cheam properties show that the house called "Whitehall" was not used as a school for the length of time previously attributed to it.[92] The Reverend George Aldrich went to Cheam in 1633 as curate, or assistant curate, to the Reverend John Hacket (1624-1662), and, probably, became established as a capable tutor there before he went to Crowborough in 1644, during the conflict between the Reverend Mr. Hacket and Cromwell's puritans over the use of the Prayer Book. He had returned from Sussex by 1646, because the Caius College Registers at Cambridge state that a Robert Angell was admitted there on 8th May, 1650, after four years at Mr. Aldrich's school in Cheam, and an Edward Farmer went to King's College in the same year, having been his pupil for three years.[79]

Probably, the Reverend Mr. Aldrich's capabilities as a tutor soon became well-known after his return to Cheam, and, with the increasing number of pupils, his income from them enabled him to lease the School House to provide adequate accommodation for them. The Surrey Hearth Tax return for 1664 credited him with fourteen, and he had the highest number of chimneys in the village that year. In the next return, for 1670, he had two returns of thirteen and seven hearths, and the latter figure could refer to those at "Whitehall". By then, his school may have expanded with the addition of many boys who were sent out of London to avoid the Plague in 1665,[79] and, possibly, he had to take some of them into his home. He died on 16th June, 1685, and left his son, George, "...all my books in my study next to my bedchamber, and all my books in my study in the school...", which indicated that he had two houses at this time and did not live in the school house. His usher, the Reverend Henry Day, succeeded him as headmaster,[79] and had bought a house in Upper Cheam in 1684 for himself, his wife and five daughters.[94, 95]

As well as owning a house of modern historical importance in Cheam, William had added enough land to his estate to cause Woodcote to be divided into Little and Greater. His 'Little Woodcot' did not appear in any documents before he lived at Woodcote Lodge, and neither was it shown on Rocque's map of 1762, therefore, the division of the area took place sometime after that year. Probably, he had purchased some, if not all, of Thomas's lands on Woodcote's western side to assist him financially.

By now, Woodcote Lodge had an inner courtyard, and the oldest section of the house included the sixteenth-century eastern wing, which was used as the kitchen quarters, with servants' bedrooms above these. An archway in the west wing provided access into the courtyard for coaches and horses, and the coachman and groom lived on the first floor over the coach-house adjacent to the stables on the southern side. The well-house and large draw-well stood at the rear of them. The Lodge's main entrance was on the western side of the front section, and all of the principal rooms here faced north, with vistas over the park towards Carshalton and Mitcham.[96] The walled garden retained its formal design,[97] and an ice-house in the grounds near there was probably constructed in William's time.

Local legend alleged that Woodcote Lodge was connected by an underground passage to the grotto in Carshalton Park. The origin of this story probably arose from the ownership of these properties by Thomas and William. The route of the passageway supposedly followed a line of old trees and, until recent years, these could be seen from the roof of the house.[96]

William's friend, Dr. Edmund Sanxay, became the owner of a considerable amount of property in Cheam.[98] He married Maria Antrobus, whose family were of some importance in the village,[11] and they had two daughters, Fanny Maria and Mary.[98] After his father died in 1757, and the subsequent death of his mother, Edmund inherited the house previously owned by the Reverend Henry Day when he was headmaster of Cheam School.[99] A few years later, Mr. Sanxay was the owner of most of the land in the square formed by the modern Ewell Road, Park Lane and The Broadway, on which he built "Cheam House", and designed a small park and pleasure grounds around it.[98] He was destined to play a significant role in events which occurred just before, and after, William's death.

As he grew older, William became absorbed with the state of his health, which led to his addiction to "quack medicines", although these did not improve his condition! In October, 1771, he sold his Cheam and Cuddington properties, including the old School House, to Edmund Sanxay, who paid £4,000 for them,[92] and added part of the School's grounds to those of "Cheam House" to provide a paddock and kitchen garden.[98] Probably, William's reason for disposing of this section of his estate was to prevent his brother, Louis, from inheriting it under the terms of their father's will!

William's health continued to deteriorate, and his addiction to the "quack medicines" met with Jane Butterfield's disapproval. Gradually,

19 (*above*): Carshalton House. It was owned by John Hodson Durand from 1792 until 1799. 20 (*below*): The Greyhound Inn at Sutton. John Hodson Durand stayed here for a few weeks before his death in February, 1830.

her role became that of a devoted nurse, but, at times, she was able to leave her patient and go out hunting with his hounds.[187] He made out a new will in 1774 in which he left £4,000 to his daughter, Mary; however, Jane persuaded him to increase the sum to £7,000.[186] He died under strange circumstances in July, 1775, and there was a considerable amount of speculation about the cause of his death.

CHAPTER 6

SUSPECTED MURDER AT WOODCOTE LODGE

Thomas Scawen died at Stone Court early in 1774, and was buried at Carshalton on 23rd February,[100] leaving his son, James, with all of his debts and depleted estates.[21] William had become seriously ill by June, 1775, allegedly from mercurial or corrosive sublimate poisoning. Finally, Edmund Sanxay took him to "Cheam House", where his death occurred on 8th July, 1775.[80] An inquest followed, and resulted in Jane Butterfield's arrest on suspicion of murder,[78] but neither Mr. Sanxay, nor any other doctor, carried out a *post mortem* on the deceased as requested by the Coroner![101] Miss Butterfield appeared before the blind magistrate, Sir John Fielding (half-brother of Henry Fielding, the novelist), and was committed to Tothillfields Bridewell to await her trial, although there was no positive evidence against her, and she repeatedly stated that she had not murdered William Scawen.[78, 88] Meanwhile, William's funeral took place on 15th July, and he joined his eldest brother in Carshalton's churchyard.[100]

Jane's imprisonment caused a sensation among the local community, and a large crowd of spectators gathered outside the court in Croydon by dawn on the day of her trial at the Assizes on Saturday, 19th August, 1775. The deputy Sheriff found places in the courtroom for "a number of handsome young ladies", then, at 7 a.m., the prisoner arrived in a post-chaise with the Keeper of Tothillfields Bridewell and a lady, who was her friend. Several of "the first families in the county paid their respects to her, lamented her unfortunate position and heartily wished her a safe deliverance". Sir Sydney Smythe, the Lord Chief Baron of the Exchequer, was the judge in charge of the proceedings, which commenced with an indictment charging Jane with administering a mixture of corrosive sublimate to William Scawen on, or between, 14th and 16th June, with "an intent to poison him", so that "he languished in great pain and torture" until 8th July, when he died at Cheam.[80]

Robert Cochran, an apothecary, was the prosecution's first witness. He attended William at the end of March, and found him with "violent" symptoms of mercurial poisoning, but these had disappeared by 17th

April after the medicine he prescribed had taken effect. On 14th May, he was called to attend the running ulcer full of "vermin or maggots" on William's arm. This had troubled him for many years, and its condition was improved with his prescription of sarsaparilla. On his next visit on 14th June, he was alarmed by the excessive salivation and "brassy taste" in Mr. Scawen's ulcerated mouth, but the prisoner assured him that no other medications had been taken by the patient, except those prescribed by him, and she had administered these herself. He began to suspect "foul play", and that the past and present troubles were caused by corrosive sublimate! His suspicions increased, and, on his way to Woodcote, he called on Lady Mead to discuss her brother's illness, and was informed she had heard that "they" were poisoning him! He requested her to ask Mr. Sanxay to call on his patient, and he had done so on the morning of 17th June. When cross-examined, Mr. Cochran stated that his shopman, William Dyer, made up the prescriptions for Mr. Scawen, and neither of these contained mercury, nor did he feel that the "quack medicines" taken before his first visit could produce such effects six weeks, or two months, afterwards.[80]

The second witness, Edmund Sanxay, confirmed that Lady Mead had requested him to call at Woodcote on 17th June, when he found the deceased suffering from a brassy taste and salivations in his ulcerated mouth. The taste disappeared after he made his patient wash out his mouth, and he suggested to the prisoner that it had been caused by something added to the liquids, but she declared that Mr. Scawen had only taken those given to him by herself. After further discussion, Mr. Sanxay told her that he would arrange for a nurse to care for William, but she protested that he would not take food or liquid from other people. However, he took this precaution and then tested the effect produced by a very small dose of corrosive sublimate on his patient's mouth – and it was the same "as that complained of when he took his draughts". He removed him to his own house in Cheam to provide him with better attention, and although his condition improved at first, including the ulcer on his arm, his ulcerated mouth "brought on a fever of mortification that terminated in his death". In Mr. Sanxay's opinion, corrosive sublimate taken in small doses could cause a person to die. He added that, after he left Woodcote, Mr. Scawen informed him that he had been poisoned. The doctor then stated that this was why he died; also William's new will made out on 22nd June, "bequeathed his fortune from the prisoner" and "gave his real estate to his heir at law".[80]

During his lengthy cross-examination, Mr. Sanxay told the court that

66

21 The Earl of Derby's Staghounds; from a painting by James Baringer (1780-1831). The background presumably is Banstead Downs with Banstead windmill (the site of Banstead Hospital) on the horizon. The huntsmen include Lord Stanley and the Hon. Edward Stanley.

none of his patients had died from ulcerated mouths and salivations. The brassy taste in Mr. Scawen's mouth disappeared after he left Woodcote, and it was impossible for a dose of mercury to produce effects again once they had ceased. William's death was caused by corrosive sublimate given to him in his liquids or "spoon meat". Finally, when asked why he had not conducted a *post mortem* if he suspected that the deceased had been poisoned, he replied that, because the doses were given in small quantities, no traces of mercury would have been visible.[80]

Mr. Young, of St. Bartholomew's Hospital, confirmed that he had been called on by Mr. Sanxay to give a second opinion on the patient. He thought Mr. Scawen's symptoms were caused by corrosive sublimate. When cross-examined about Mr. Cochran's mercurial ointment prescribed for the deceased's ulcerated arm, and whether it could have adverse effects on him because it contained mercury, he replied that it would depend on the quantity in the prescription. He was of the opinion that the patient's symptoms arose from mercurial poisoning and, if the doses had been large enough, the cause of his death could have been revealed by a *post mortem*.[80]

William's carter, Wheelock, described to the court how he had taken two bottles of the rheumatic tincture (quack medicine) from Harris's of St. Paul's Churchyard, so that his master could see what adverse effects, if any, were produced by it – and there were none! He was followed by a Dr. Saunders, in whose opinion the symptoms described previously were those of mercurial poisoning, but he admitted on cross-examination that Maredant's or Norton's drops taken in large quantities would have the same effect. Another servant, Robert Erle, said he had purchased three bottles of the tincture from Harris', who informed him that it did contain mercury. Once or twice in February he had seen Mr. Scawen drink some medicine from a square bottle kept in a closet adjoining his study; also he had taken him some gruel prepared by the cook, when his immediate servant, Emor, and Miss Butterfield were both absent.[80]

The proprietor of the tincture, William Dodd, stated that there was no mercury in it, but, when cross-examined, admitted that he did not have any specification of its contents. The bookseller, Harris, who sold the mixture, knew nothing of its composition, and Dr. Higgins, who examined it, could not find any mercury in it, although he said his analysis could not be completely relied upon, because it was used only to discover the common mixture of mercury usually contained in quack medicines. In his cross-examination, he stated that a very small quantity of mercury would have "powerful effects" on somebody in a weak condition; also, he understood that Maredant's drops did not contain any, and the bottle analysed had been purchased "after the affair of poison was first spoken of". The chemist, Mr. Godfrey, confirmed these statements, and said that the medicine had been bought on 28th July, when the prisoner was in Tothillfields Bridewell.[80]

Robert Erle was requested to return to the witness box, and said that he purchased the bottles of medicine about one week after Mr. Scawen's death. The mixture he had seen his master take from the square bottle was reddish in colour, and stained both the cup and the spoon. Then Emor confirmed that he gave Wheelock the tincture, and he took "a bottle and a half of it" without any ill-effects. He did not remember his master taking bottles out of the closet, or that their contents made him sick, and added that all of Mr. Scawen's foods and liquids were given to him by the prisoner, who "behaved very well towards the deceased, was extremely careful and tender, and used to dress his wounds or sores".[80]

The gardener, William Walker, said that before Mr. Scawen went to Cheam, he had heard the prisoner say to him: "You shall not go, I will not permit it", and his master replied: "Would you have me stay? I believe you mean to kill me quite. Would you have me stay to be poisoned?" Also, he had refused her request for some beer, sherry, wine and money. When cross-examined, Walker told the court that Jane had suggested visits to the deceased at Mr. Sanxay's home, but his master's reply was: "No, my dear, do not come to me, when I am well, I will come to you". The coachman, Joseph Cantwell, confirmed the other servants' evidence, and all of them agreed that Mr. Scawen's attitude towards Miss Butterfield arose from the suggestion made by Mr. Sanxay that she had poisoned him, because before then, she had been treated by him "in the most respectful, endearing and affectionate manner".[80]

Mr. Cochran's shopman, William Dyer, was the prosecution's last witness, and stated that Mr. Scawen's medicine prescribed by Mr. Cochran did not contain any mercury. The evidence for the prosecution had taken about four hours to present to the court and, at approximately 11 a.m., Miss Butterfield was asked what she had to say in her defence, but she was too overcome to read this out. A clerk received permission to do so on her behalf, and described how she had been taken from her parents at the age of fourteen, and brought to Mr. Scawen, who persuaded her to live with him, although "the circumstances broke her father's heart". The deceased had given her every kindness and spared no expense on her education. She had grown to love him, "and had, by a conduct of many years, convinced him of her affection and gratitude". She had nursed him during the six years of his illness, and given him constant attention and care by day and night, so that she could administer his food and medicines to him. The whole family, and other people in the neighbourhood, received her as "Mrs. Scawen". She added that she had sincerely loved him, and hoped that, taking everything into consideration, nobody would believe that she was capable of murdering her "best benefactor".[80]

Another surgeon, Mr. Bromfield, was the first defence witness, and stated that the effects of mercury could return without more of it being taken. From his experience of such cases, he was astonished that anyone could have doubts about this fact, and quoted several cases in which patients had died in circumstances similar to those described by Mr. Sanxay. Dr. Brocklesby confirmed Mr. Bromfield's testimony, and added that the effects of mercury on any person would depend on the condition and strength of the patient, but it was impossible to administer corrosive sublimate without the patient's knowledge, and he had confirmed his opinion by an experiment on himself. Also, if traces of mercury were present, these could be washed from the roots of the tongue when liquid was swallowed, and produce the brassy taste "so much relied upon by the gentlemen of the other side".[80]

Confirmation of Dr. Brocklesby's evidence was given by two other surgeons, Mr. Howard and Dr. Ingram, who also knew of instances where mercury had been active again after two or three weeks. Another surgeon, Mr. Perry, agreed with them, and quoted from "two or three very curious cases". He had advised the deceased about "some of those quack nostrums". When he had analysed the rheumatic tincture, he found that it did contain a great quantity of mercury. Another witness, the Reverend Mr. Lodge, said that, frequently, he had been present when the prisoner tried to dissuade Mr. Scawen from taking the quack medicines. Also, he gave Miss Butterfield "the most favourable character".[80]

Another doctor, Mr. Townsend, confirmed that the deceased constantly dosed himself with the tincture. Mr. Scawen was in a very emaciated condition when he dined at Mr. Townsend's house in April, and had said that he feared he had been poisoned by the quack medicines. Townsend had ended his evidence by giving "the best character to the prisoner".[80]

The last witness for the defence, Miss Smith, agreed with both the Reverend Mr. Lodge and Mr. Townsend about the prisoner's good

22 (*above*): The interior of the Carshalton Cricket Bowl. The cricket scene, Mr. Durand's initials (J.D.) and the date of presentation, 1796, are shown in the medallion on the base. 23 (*below*): The exterior of the Carshalton Cricket Bowl, showing one of the three groups of flowers and fruit.

character, and the "care, affection and tenderness" she gave to the deceased. She stated that Miss Butterfield had continually complained to Mr. Scawen about his addiction to the rheumatic tincture, and pointed out that, after his death, she could have easily absconded. However, it had been most difficult to persuade her to move from Woodcote to the deceased's lodgings in Somerset House, and when she left them, she had informed everyone of her new address.

The evidence ended at approximately 2 p.m., and the judge took an hour and a half in which to sum up the whole proceedings. The jury retired, but returned after only fifteen minutes with their verdict of "not guilty", and their decision was followed by tremendous applause from the spectators! The crowd outside the court unhorsed Miss Butterfield's carriage and took her in a triumphant procession through Croydon. Afterwards, a banquet was given in her honour at the George Hotel and, when they had dined, the ladies of the party set out for London at 6 p.m. in post-chaises-and-four, with an escort of gentlemen on horseback.[88] A report of the trial with a full-length engraving of Jane on that day, appeared in the *Lady's Magazine* for August, 1775.[80] There can be no doubt that the majority of people both inside, and outside, the courtroom believed in Jane's innocence. However, for over two hundred years, it has also been alleged that her freedom was due to the aptitude of her counsel.

William Scawen knew the true cause of his illness and, probably, was not fully convinced that Jane had poisoned him. In his will dated 22nd June, 1775, he gave £10,000 to his daughter, Mary, and left his personal estate to her male heirs, or, if none, to his nephew, James, in tail-male, but did not mention his real estate. Perhaps he hoped that Miss Butterfield could claim something after his death to repay her for her years of devotion to him? However, on 25th June, 1775, Mr. Sanxay made him add a codecil, in which he stated that some doubts might arise because he had not mentioned his real estate in his will, therefore, he revoked all former wills made out by him.[90]

Miss Butterfield had been friendly with a Captain Moss for about eighteen months before William's death. He had visited her at Woodcote Lodge with Mr. Scawen's consent, and it was understood that they would be married. William had made out a will in August, 1774, in which he left a considerable amount of property to Jane; therefore, if her marriage took place after he died, his real estate would pass into the Captain's ownership. Thus, while Mr. Scawen was at Mr. Sanxay's home, the surgeon made sure that an attorney, Mr. William Pellatt, received instructions to remove Jane from Woodcote Lodge, but she had refused to leave there until permission was given for her to stay at the rooms in Somerset House. When William Scawen died, she was subjected to slanderous statements made by Edmund Sanxay and others, who ensured that the newspapers had their share of the story.[186]

The truth about William's illness was not widely published, or mentioned in the *Lady's Magazine*, probably to avoid causing any further embarrassment to his family. Consequently, more gossip and scandal about the affair circulated throughout Surrey's "county set" in the two years after Miss Butterfield's trial. These unsatisfactory circumstances prompted one of the defence medical witnesses, Mr. Ingram, to produce a book about the case. He was a surgeon at Christ's Hospital, with experience in cases of sublimate poisoning, and there was no doubt whatsoever in his mind that Jane was innocent. His book, published in 1777, gave a "strict and impartial" inquiry into the cause and death of "the late William Scawen Esquire of Woodcote Lodge in Surrey..."[101] Possibly, it was too outspoken at that time, and nobody dared to admit to any knowledge of its contents; thus, the facts about Mr. Scawen's ailment have not been widely known.

Mr. Ingram began his "inquiry" by examining the evidence of Robert Cochran, an apothecary from Mitcham. Mr. Cochran had stated that, on 2nd April, 1775, he had called to see his patient, Mr. Scawen, and found that he was suffering from a swollen face; bad breath; excessive salivations caused by a badly ulcerated mouth, in which he had a "brassy taste"; his eyes were sore and he was almost blind; also he was in a poor physical condition. The apothecary thought that William Scawen was in the "utmost danger", and was told by him that these symptoms had been caused by the rheumatic tincture which he had taken in March.[101]

Mr. Cochran said that the spreading ulcer on Mr. Scawen's arm was full of maggots, therefore he had prescribed an ointment containing "Mercurials" for it. Mr. Ingram stressed the fact that Miss Butterfield had the unpleasant task of picking out these maggots every twelve hours when a new dressing was applied! Surprisingly, the apothecary claimed that he had cured his patient in two weeks, so that Mr. Scawen was able to walk around his garden at Woodcote Lodge and travel a distance of about thirteen miles to London, where he visited a Dr. James and a Mr. John Townsend, with whom he stayed for three days, and, except for the brassy taste in his mouth, he was very well![101]

However, Mr. Ingram pointed out that Mr. Scawen's quack medicine did not contain any mercury. His carter, Wheelock, had taken one and a half bottles of the mixture under Mr. Cochran's supervision, and no ill effects were produced by it. Mr. Dodd, the proprietor of the tincture, had sworn on oath that it had no mercury in it, and the two eminent chemists, Dr. Higgins and Dr. Godfrey, had reached the same conclusion after they had analysed it at Sir John Fielding's request. The true cause of William Scawen's illness and the ulcer on his arm was venereal disease.[101]

Mr. Cochran had admitted his inexperience in respect of the effects produced by mercury, and he had no knowledge whatsoever about venereal disease, but, said Mr. Ingram, he did have a good opinion of his own medical capabilities! He could have learnt the cause of his patient's illness from Edmund Sanxay, but hostile feelings arose between the surgeon and the apothecary after Mr. Sanxay had not ordered any medicines for Mr. Scawen from Mr. Cochran's shop from 4th May to 17th June.[101]

Mr. Ingram said that, probably, Mr. Cochran's quick cure he had provided for Mr. Scawen in April was due to the fact that he realised that his other prescription of a white powder called "Calomel" for Mr. Scawen's ulcer had bad effects on the patient, and, therefore, did not prescribe any more for him because it contained mercury. Mr. Cochran also thought that the rheumatic tincture was the cause of his patient's other symptoms, but this was not true. Mr. Scawen had suffered from these disorders for years due to his venereal disease, and they "portend approaching Death..."[101]

Mr. Ingram said that Mr. Cochran changed his opinion about the poisonous quality of the rheumatic tincture after he paid a friendly visit to Mr. Scawen on 16th June. On his way home from Woodcote, he had called on Lady Mead and told her that her brother was very ill, and he believed that Mr. Scawen's condition was caused by mercurial poisoning (ratsbane) and not by the quack medicines. He asked her to obtain Mr. Sanxay's opinion about her brother's illness and also informed her that it seemed likely that "foul Play and unfair Methods" had been used on her brother. Mr. Ingram then pointed out that on this day, "Corrosive Sublimate had its Birth".[101]

Lady Mead took Mr. Cochran's advice, and, on the next day, she spoke to Mr. Sanxay when he passed by her house on his way to Woodcote. She asked the surgeon to tell her his opinion of her brother's condition, but, before he had time to reply, she informed him that "they" were poisoning William by giving him corrosive sublimate. Edmund Sanxay had admitted that he was surprised by her statement

24 One of the lavender fields at Little Woodcote, 1908. The woods on the left-hand side mark the southern boundary of Woodcote Hall's parklands. The houses in the background are at Woodcote Green.

and wondered how she had obtained this information. However, he had no knowledge of Lady Mead's conversation with Mr. Cochran, whose rash statements had caused her such distress. In Mr. Ingram's opinion, the apothecary's first duty was to inform Mr. Sanxay of his suspicions about the poison allegedly being administered to Mr. Scawen, who was in Mr. Sanxay's sole care, but he resented the fact that the surgeon had not ordered any medicines from his shop for a period of six weeks. Surely, someone who was suspicious that his friend was being murdered would not withhold the information for days, thus giving the murderer time to finish off his victim! Also, how did Mr. Cochran reach the conclusion that sublimate was being used to kill someone whom he had not been allowed to visit professionally for a month – and the apothecary had been in Brighthelmstone [Brighton] for part of that time![101]

Mr. Ingram pointed out that an accusation of murder usually had some kind of proof to substantiate it, but this was not given at the trial. During Mr. Scawen's long and painful illness, he had not presented one important symptom of corrosive sublimate poisoning. Therefore, Mr. Cochran's statement about the poison could only be classed as a "wild accusation", because he had given up his opinion of the poisonous contents of Mr. Scawen's quack medicines by the time of his visit to Lady Mead on 16th June.[101]

Next, Mr. Ingram examined the evidence given by Mr. Sanxay and another apothecary, Mr. Read. On 4th May, Mr. Sanxay had been called to attend to the ulcer on Mr. Scawen's arm, and found that it was in such a bad condition it gave his room an almost unbearable smell. In Mr. Sanxay's opinion, it was a venereal ulcer which had slowly increased in size over a number of years, and his patient's eye trouble was due to the same disease. Mr. Sanxay had prescribed mercury for Mr. Scawen at one time, but found that he was allergic to it, and this fact had been confirmed by Mr. Read.[101]

Mr. Ingram said that Mr. Read's prescription of a light milk diet and sarsaparilla from 4th May to 2nd June had improved Mr. Scawen's condition, and Mr. Read advised him to continue with the diet until 14th June. On that day, Mr. Read found that Mr. Scawen was feverish and suffered from a sore mouth, swollen gums, more ulcers on the inside of his lips and excessive salivation. In Mr. Ingram's opinion, there could be no doubt that William Scawen had entered the final stages of venereal disease, and his death was imminent. If a cure had been found for the disease at that time, all of his symptoms would have vanished. By 16th June, he was too ill to travel to Mr. Sanxay's house in Cheam, and the surgeon had to call on him at Woodcote Lodge.[101]

On 16th June, when Mr. Cochran told Lady Mead that her brother was being poisoned, Mr. Sanxay informed his patient that he did not know the cause of the brassy taste in his mouth. Therefore, said Mr. Ingram, although the apothecary stated that poison had been given to Mr. Scawen, the surgeon did not attribute his patient's illness to that cause! However, on 17th June, when Mr. Scawen's condition had deteriorated, and after Lady Mead's conversation with Mr. Sanxay, when Mr. Cochran's "Alarm took Blaze", the surgeon suddenly changed his diagnosis and proceeded to tell his patient that he had been poisoned. Jane Butterfield said that it was impossible for any of the servants at Woodcote Lodge to have committed such a crime – but she did not realise that she was the person who would be accused of it![101]

Mr. Ingram said that Mr. Sanxay persisted with his accusations about the poison on the next day, 18th June, but Mr. Scawen rejected the idea that the contents of his drinking bowl had contained corrosive sublimate, and said that the brassy taste was due to the bad condition of his mouth; also the bowl's contents sometimes tasted normal and the bowl was never out of his sight. In Mr. Ingram's opinion, these rational answers were important and proved the patient's knowledge of the cause of his symptoms. If sublimate had been added, even in small doses, to the liquid in the bowl, it would produce the same taste at all times. The liquid did not contain any poison, because the silver spoons used to administer it, and the silver saucepan in which it was heated, did not discolour. Mr. Scawen's gold watch, gold ring, and the guineas in his pocket, had not turned white through contact with him. The hounds and the domestic dogs and cats, who licked up any small quantity of the liquid, had not presented symptoms of poisoning. If the doctors were so suspicious of the contents of the bowl, Mr. Ingram wondered why they had never tasted them. He also pointed out that when Mr. Scawen cleansed his mouth, or gargled, the brassy taste disappeared, and this proved that the liquids were not poisoned.[101]

Corrosive sublimate cannot be given as a slow poison, said Mr. Ingram, even by the most skilful person, and certainly not by a young woman. It acts very quickly and causes severe pains in the stomach, which becomes distended, with damaged linings. Until these symptoms have been produced, it cannot cause a sore mouth. The only symptom in Mr. Scawen's stomach was described as an "uneasiness" produced by the unclean condition of his mouth. After death, the body turns a livid colour with large blotches on it, but no *post mortem* had been carried out on Mr. Scawen, nor his body's condition observed as requested by the coroner at the inquest. The doctors concerned in the case had stated that the small doses of poison would have disappeared due to the time lapse between death and examination, but in Mr. Ingram's opinion, their statements were untrue. He quoted from a case in which the victim's body had been opened twenty days after he had died, and signs of corrosive sublimate were easily seen. Therefore, Mr. Scawen's body should have been inspected to prove whether he had, or had not, been poisoned.[101]

Mr. Ingram pointed out that if corrosive sublimate had been administered to Mr. Scawen, it would have cured the ulcer on his arm and killed the vermin in it. The "Blackeries Lixivitium" prescribed for him by Mr. Sanxay on 17th June should have given him relief instead of making him violently sick, because it was a very good antidote for this type of poison. Jane Butterfield had been accused of poisoning Mr. Scawen's "Bark Draught", but the patient had always seen the cork taken out of the bottle and watched her pour the medicine into his cup. He also insisted that he would be able to eat if his mouth was in a better condition, and this was proved correct when the ulcers temporarily disappeared.[101]

Mr. Ingram wondered what motives Mr. Sanxay had for keeping his suspicions about the poison to himself, if he had any, for so many days, and why did he not tell Lady Mead about them when she informed him that sublimate was being given to her brother? All of Mr. Sanxay's evidence on that subject was very curious, and so was Mr. Young's second opinion on Mr. Scawen. Mr. Young had seen the patient on one occasion only, and that visit occurred after Mr. Cochran's conversation with Lady Mead. William Scawen had been forced to suffer from his distressing symptoms without the proper medications for them during the continual discussions about the poisoning.

Mr. Sanxay had great difficulty in trying to convince Mr. Scawen that Jane Butterfield was guilty, because he repeatedly insisted that it was impossible for her to administer poison to him. However, said Mr. Ingram, once the patient had been removed to Sanxay's house, he was made to believe her guilt. Meanwhile, Mrs. Sanxay was forced to leave her home because she could not bear Mr. Scawen's horrible symptoms, and the smell from the dressing on his ulcer. After Edmund Sanxay had altered William Scawen's opinion about Miss Butterfield, he very quickly made him alter his will and cut out his bequest to her![101] (Mr. Ingram did not know of Mr. Sanxay's difficulties in trying to make Mr.

25 (*above*): The earliest railway station at Wallington. 26 (*below*): Woodcote Road, looking south from the railway bridge. The photograph was taken before any of the shops had been built.

Scawen mention his real estate in that document.)

Mr. Ingram quoted from various cases of mercurial poisoning to show the possibility that Mr. Cochran's prescriptions of "Mercury and Calomel" for Mr. Scawen's ulcer had adverse effects on the patient because of his weak condition. He also emphasised that, from the time of her appearance before Sir John Fielding, Jane Butterfield had repeatedly insisted that neither she, nor any of the servants at Woodcote Lodge, could have administered poison to Mr. Scawen. His "inquiry" ended with the hope that his statements would alleviate the malignant and untrue stories which were circulating throughout most of Surrey, and then he gave details of post mortems he had carried out on several cases of mercurial poisoning when he had found evidence of the cause of death.[101]

In 1777, Jane Butterfield contested the validity of Mr. Scawen's will, which he had made out with Mr. Sanxay's help.[78] However, there are no notes on this document to prove that she was successful in her attempt to regain something from his estate as a reward for her years of devotion to a man who, at the end of his life, was too frail and ill to defend her against the serious accusation of poisoning him.

There can be no doubt that there was some "foul play and unfair methods" in this strange affair, but not in the context of Mr. Cochran's accusation, which, probably was made to divert any blame from his prescriptions, which produced adverse effects on Mr. Scawen. If he wished to damage Mr. Sanxay's reputation after he ceased to order any medicines from his shop, he also provided this doctor and others with an opportunity to use his ignorance in respect of mercurial poisoning and venereal disease, and the fact that William Scawen was dying. Jane Butterfield had originated from the lower classes, who were considered expendable in those days. Apart from any money she was due to inherit on William's death, the real estate he had left her, and her impending marriage to Captain Moss, were sufficient to cause a good deal of alarm and jealousy among her benefactor's relatives. Clearly, someone was determined that she would not become the owner of Woodcote Lodge!

William's daughter, Mary, who resided with a Mrs. Withers at East Grinstead at the time of her father's death, became a wealthy young woman when his will was proved.[90] Previously, her meagre income had been supplemented by presents of money from Jane Butterfield.[186] Woodcote Lodge and Little Woodcote passed to Louis Scawen and remained in his possession until 1786, with Mr. William Pellatt as the rated occupier of them.[102] Louis acted as the executor of Robert

Scawen's will in 1778, in which the Reigate estates were left in trust to be sold for the benefit of his daughter, Louisa.[11] By November, 1782, Louis was the surviving legatee named in Sir Thomas's will, and was granted administration of the goods, chattels and credits left unadministered by the sole executrix, Dame Martha.[76]

James Scawen, who was due to inherit his Uncle William's personal estate if his illegitimate cousin, Mary, had no male heirs,[90] apparently spent most of his time in Maidwell in Northamptonshire.[104] He was unable to repay the large debts left to him by his father, Thomas, despite having sold some of his properties to raise the necessary money. Therefore, on 20th April, 1779, those left unsold were put in trust for sale to secure £40,000 and interest,[103] and this mortgage was foreclosed in 1782. Afterwards, the remainder of the property was sold off in lots, so that, finally, the trustees were left with £3,625. When he died in 1800, his body was returned to Carshalton and buried in the churchyard there.[21]

CHAPTER 7

THE GEORGIAN MILLIONAIRE

Apparently, William Pellatt leased Woodcote Lodge and Little Woodcote to a Mr. Wood during the period in which he was the rated occupier of them.[105] Mr. Pellatt's name frequently appears in documents connected with local history, but very little is known about him. He was an attorney employed by Sir Nicholas Hacket Carew, whose will dated 1st July, 1762, described him as a "gentleman of Morden".[106] After Sir Nicholas's death at the beginning of August, 1762, he administered his estates as locum lord of the manors involved[107] for approximately another eighteen years, and paid the rents from Beddington to the ailing Catherine Carew, provided she obeyed the wishes expressed in her father's will, and remained a spinster because of her infirmity (whatever this was). On her marriage, or death, all of the properties were to pass to the male heir of Dr. John Fountain, the Dean of York, or, if none, then to William Farrer's eldest son, and, lastly, to Richard Gee of Orpington, who was Philippa Carew's grandson and, with the failure of the two lines mentioned, the nearest Beddington Carew relative.[11, 26]

Mr. Pellatt had moved to Croydon by 1764, when Miss Carew made out her will and named him as sole executor.[108] She died unmarried in 1769, and, afterwards, the death of Dr. Fountain's son occurred in 1780, before he reached the age of twenty-five and could receive his inheritance. Mr. Farrer had no male heir, and the estates passed to Richard Gee, who took the name and arms of Carew.[26] Meanwhile, William Pellatt was involved in Carshalton's affairs as one of the trustees for the Fellowes' Charity in 1776.[109] His involvement with Woodcote Lodge and Little Woodcote ended early in 1786, but he administered some lands in Greater Woodcote until Richard Gee Carew's brother, William, took these over in 1795.[102]

By May 1786, Louis Scawen had sold Woodcote Lodge and Little Woodcote to John Durand,[109] who was a very wealthy man of unknown origins, whose fortune had been made through his employment with the East India Company.[84] He had lived in Carshalton for about twenty-five years,[89] during which time he gained a notoriety for his love of hunting

27 (*above*): The east drive from Woodcote Hall, looking towards Woodcote Road.
28 (*below*): The same scene, taken from Woodcote Road after the east drive became
Woodcote Avenue in about 1912.

and horse-racing,[78] and, probably, these sporting interests influenced him when he decided to buy the mansion and its estate. Another more famous sportsman, Edward, the twelfth Earl of Derby, now used "The Oaks" as his sporting seat, and had inaugurated two famous races on the adjacent Downs between Woodmansterne and Epsom: the Oaks in 1779, and the Derby in 1780.[67]

John was born in 1719, spent most of his early career at sea in the East India Company's service, and rose to the rank of Captain.[84] Then he lived in Bengal,[110] where the Company had its headquarters and gave him the opportunity to meet other notable men in the same employment. They made their fortunes from the flourishing trade in cotton, silk yarn, sugar, and the saltpetre used in the wars of that time. All of these items came from the rich, extensive hinterland there. Many employees returned to England, lost their money, and went back for more,[111] but John's fortune was wisely invested when he came to this country in 1760-61, probably with Lord Clive. He set himself up as a London merchant at 51, Lime Street, and, later, went into partnership with a William Nixon at Greenland Dock in Rotherhithe. Their business prospered and was extended to the Lime Street address.[84, 110]

After he arrived in Carshalton in 1761, John resided at Bornheim House, which, probably, stood on the site of the approach road to the railway station in North Street, and was owned by Henry Byne.[71] He quickly established himself on the local scene, became a landowner, and leased land from others, including Thomas and William Scawen.[89] He also took an active part in parish affairs, and was made an Overseer of the Poor in 1762/3 and 1765; a Surveyor in 1767, 1769, and 1781; Officer of the Parish in 1776; and was elected for the Fellowes' Trust on 23rd January, 1788.[109]

Similarly to his wealthy contemporaries with fortunes made in the East India Company's service, John desired the social standing and prestige which could be obtained with his money, and "a seat in Parliament, like an estate in the country, became a symbol of success"! He began his political career in 1767 by canvassing for a seat in Worcestershire, which was a stronghold of the Company's men, and his election campaign met with their disapproval! On 25th November, 1767, John Walsh wrote to Lord Clive: "What think you of Mr. Durand? He has had the folly and impertinence to talk loudly about Worcester; he is now set out for Totnes"![84]

Undaunted by cool receptions in both Worcester and Totnes, John continued his election campaign elsewhere, and, allegedly, offered

£4,000 for a borough seat; but he gained a strong foothold in Aylesbury a few weeks before the voting took place! Unfortunately, he upset another of the East India Company's men, Sir Eyre Coote, who hoped to obtain that seat as a supporter of John Wilkes, the other Member there,[84] then imprisoned in the Tower for daring to criticise George III in an article in the *North Briton*, which he owned and edited.[12] In February, 1768, Sir Eyre wrote to another of Wilkes' supporters, Sir William Lee, and complained that Durand was "fully determined to get into the House at any rate, provided money can effect it"![84]

After he obtained his seat in the Commons, John kept a low profile and did not vote until 1769.[84] The Wilkes affair had yet to be resolved without upsetting his supporters in the lower classes. Finally, the matter was settled when his private life of debauchery, and his parody of Pope's *Essay on Man*, entitled *Essay on Woman*, were used against him, resulting in his loss of popularity and expulsion from the House.[12] John's first votes on 27th January and 2nd February, 1769, were for Wilkes, but on 3rd February, he voted with the Government to expel him, and supported the Administration for the remainder of his time in office.[84]

Before the next election, John tried to stand again as a Member for Aylesbury, but was defeated. After an unsuccessful campaign at Honiton in Devon, he was returned to Parliament as the Government candidate for Plympton through the influence of Lord Edgcumbe,[84] who was an Admiral and the Treasurer of the Royal Household.[12] John's lack of activity in Parliament's next session displeased another of his colleagues in the East India Company, John Robinson, who looked after the Company's stockholders' interests in the Commons. In an undated letter to the First Lord of the Admiralty, the Earl of Sandwich, Mr. Robinson remarked: "Durand was 'remarkably slack' and could not be depended on". However, in 1780, Mr. Durand's name appeared in five division lists, and he voted each time for the Administration. In the same year, the Opposition newspaper wrote scathingly of him: "No man understands the 'Multiplication Table' with more comprehensiveness and precision of intelligence; but in the laws of his country, or in the duties of a legislator, there is perhaps no individual more completely ignorant"![84]

John was not put forward again as the Treasury (i.e. government) candidate for Plympton, and he planned to oppose the Fane candidates at Lyme, but Lord North warned him to keep away from there. Lyme was a borough with two parliamentary seats, and only fifty voters, entirely controlled by the tenth Earl of Westmorland, through his family whose name was Fane, in the second half of the eighteenth century.[12, 84] John was returned to the Commons on the Treasury's interest for Seaford in Sussex, in what were said to be "circumstances which have not been explained"! During his last four years as a Member he supported Lord North, until he fell from power, and then the Earl of Sandwich; although two days before an important division on a motion to end the war in America, the Earl told John Robinson he would write to "Durand – all the rest of my friends are so orthodox that any application from me seems superfluous"![84]

On 18th February, 1783, John voted against Shelburne's peace proposals for ending the American war, and was absent from the House on 27th November when a vote was taken on Fox's East India Bill, but John Robinson classed him as one of the stockholders who were against it. Mr. Durand's dubious political career ended in 1784, when he did not stand again for re-election. There is no record to show that he made one speech during his fifteen years in Parliament,[84] but he achieved his ambition to gain his "symbol of success"! Perhaps, contrary to the Opposition newspaper's beliefs, he followed the old proverb's advice of "a still tongue in a wise head"?

Meanwhile, John's successful business life expanded considerably after he applied for a contract for victualling the troops in the ceded West Indian islands gained from France. He took this over in 1770 from his Aylesbury colleague in Parliament, Anthony Bacon. In 1772, he obtained another contract to supply the navy with masts and, during the American war, he gained more contracts both there and in the West Indies,[84] which explains why he voted against Shelburne's peace proposals in 1783.

Probably, John's love of hunting and horse-racing inspired him to buy the Greyhound at Carshalton in 1773 from another London merchant, John Mills. He was admitted as the customary tenant of the premises at a special Court Baron of Thomas Scawen held on 8th November, 1773, and paid a yearly rent of four shillings and ten pence, with a fine of £42 for his admission.[78] The inn was run for him by Michael Turner, whose widow, Deborah, took over from him after his death. Since the early part of the eighteenth century, this establishment had been a well-known venue for cock-fights and betting. There was stabling for forty hunters; also the horses entered for the races on Banstead Downs were available for inspection here.[71]

As well as his political, sporting, and business activities, John found time for more philanthropic duties. His connections with the French

Protestants in England led to his appointment as director of their hospital in Old Street, London, in 1769. His long-standing association with the Trinity House Corporation was rewarded in 1775 with promotion from the Younger to Elder Brethren,[84] which was a position of no mean honour, because these gentlemen were (and still are) chosen from members of the Royal Family, statesmen, retired naval officers of high rank, and prominent officers of the mercantile marine. The Corporation's premises were situated at Water Lane, Deptford, at that time, and it had more responsibilities then, including the suppression of piracy and fair distribution of profits accrued from dues, which were spent in charity. Also, bequests in the Elder Brethrens' wills provided one source of income for the one hundred and eleven almshouses occupied by elderly mariners, their wives, widows or unmarried daughters.[112] John's concern for the welfare of elderly, retired seamen resulted in his appointment as a director of the Greenwich Hospital in 1781,[84] where there was accommodation for two thousand and seven hundred pensioners, and it was run on similar lines to those of the Chelsea Hospital for soldiers.[113]

John's involvement with the Greenwich Hospital brought him into contact with a notable architect, surveyor and civil engineer of Scottish origin, Robert Mylne, who had been the hospital's Clerk of Works since 1775, and whose most serious competitors were the famous Adam brothers and George Dance the Younger.[114] A few years later, Mr. Mylne's work had an important place in the history of Woodcote Lodge and Little Woodcote, and associations with other buildings in Carshalton. In 1781, he surveyed a Mr. Cox's house in "Hine Street", London, for John, settled the value of the premises with a Mr. Crunden on 18th January, 1782, and it was sold to "Mr. Durund" for £1,550.[114] Probably, it was situated in present-day Hinde Street, W.1., which then was near one of London's centres of social life, the twelfth Earl of Derby's town-house in Grosvenor Square.[115] On 15th June, 1782, Mr. Mylne met John in Carshalton, and went with him to a farm in Potters Lane (modern-day whereabouts uncertain), where he surveyed the house, offices and outhouses, recommended some alterations and repairs, and gave instructions to the workmen there. He surveyed the Greyhound Inn on 9th March, 1787, because repairs and alterations were needed on it. Two plans for the work with "longwritten particulars" were submitted on 15th May, but did not meet with John's approval, and more plans were dispatched to him on 2nd August.[114] No further mention of the inn appeared in Mr. Mylne's diary, and it must be

29 (*left*): Little Woodcote farm, Woodmansterne Lane (looking west towards Little Woodcote Lane), 1921. The farmhouse is on the left behind the trees and opposite the barn. The signpost on the right indicates the bridleway to Carshalton (now the track across the smallholdings). 30 (*right*): The same scene viewed from further back up the hill.

31 Little Woodcote farm, Woodmansterne Lane (looking east up the hill towards Woodcote Green). The photograph was taken beside the old barn shown in 29 and 30.

left to conjecture as to whether his suggested improvements were carried out.

Although John retired from Parliament in 1784, he continued to attend the Carshalton Vestry meetings. By September of that year, a Mr. William Smearley had preferred an indictment against the parish's inhabitants for not keeping the Shaw Lane (Green Wrythe Lane) to Morden in good repair. Never in living memory had the ratepayers been forced to bear the expense of such repairs, only those whose properties were adjacent to the lane! The parish had already had a fine of £100 imposed on it for failure to complete other necessary work in Spartlemy Green Lane (Wrythe Lane) when one of the mill owners, Mr. Shepley, grew tired of complaining about the bad condition of the road he used, and had proceeded with his indictment. The solicitors, Messrs. Tudman and Wegener, were instructed to defend this case, and the penalty had been reduced to £90. Therefore, after Mr. Smearley's action, more discussions were held about the need to raise another £400, and John Durand and William Andrews were directed to assess each inhabitant's "rent great and small", which would be collected by John Alfrey and John Piercy. Also, it was agreed to apply to the Quarter Sessions for permission to levy a rate of nine pence in the pound.[109]

On 10th April, 1785, Mr. Wegener informed the Vestry meeting that when he had applied for an extension to be granted for Mr. Smearley's indictment at the last general Quarter Sessions at Reigate, another fine of £210 had been imposed on the parish in addition to the previous £90. Consequently, it was agreed that a rate of one shilling and nine pence was required to meet the extra costs. One week later, Messrs. Durand and Andrews were asked to give the management of the highway repairs to John Holden, who had offered to superintend them. The matter was finalised on 3rd October, 1785, so that the fines, contractor's charges and solicitors' bills could be paid. However, the discussions about the repairs did not take place in the Vestry, and proved expensive due to the thirst engendered by the participants, who were told that no more money would be paid for "any Business that is done at any Publick House", and the present "Church Wardens, Overseers and Surveyors be desired to account for what money they have now"![109]

After John bought Woodcote Lodge and Little Woodcote, he caused more anguish at the Vestry meetings when a decision was made to increase his rates! At the meeting on 15th May, 1786, he declared "that the terms and extent of his purchase were not known to himself", therefore the matter was postponed until he could provide more details about his properties. Similar to all good ratepayers, he tried to delay the increased payments for as long as possible, and was absent from the Vestry for nearly a year! Finally, on 7th May, 1787, the Committee decided: "That Mr. Durand's land in this Parish which now stands at £100 per year, is fixed at £150 per year",[109] but the ratepayer's indignation was not recorded!

In addition to his Surrey properties, John owned the advowson of the church in Bredon, Worcestershire, which he bought from Benjamin Pearkes in 1783-4. He became the owner of the rectory and living there in 1785. Probably, the cold reception given to him by his colleagues in the East India Company when he first campaigned for a seat in Parliament, made him determined to gain a foothold in the county at the end of his political career!

John remained a bachelor throughout his life; nevertheless, after his arrival in Carshalton, he set up his own family as the results of his affairs with different ladies who, probably, were employed as his servants. He took charge of his illegitimate offspring and gave them his name. Possibly, his eldest son and daughter, John and Anne, were born before he left India, and two more sons and four daughters appeared after his return to England! By August, 1785, John junior had retired from his career as Commander of the "Northington East India Ship"; John Hodsdon Durand was a second mate on another East Indiaman commanded by Captain Mackintosh, and Matthew was preparing for his ordination in the Church at the Reverend Thomas Watson's in Whitby, Yorkshire. Anne and Elizabeth lived with their father at Bornheim House, and the three younger girls, Charlotte, Jane and Sarah, resided at the fashionable Misses Ray and Fry's Boarding School in Streatham.[110] A son, James, was born on 13th April, 1775, to John Durand and Jane Matthews,[78, 117] but he was not mentioned in Mr. Durand's will made out on 1st August, 1785, and either he had died by then, or he was the result of John junior's affair with this lady.

After John moved to Woodcote Lodge early in 1786, he entertained his hunting and racing friends there. Each year, when the sporting season began, the surrounding countryside was the scene of "perpetual activity", which included field sports and the horse-races on the Downs at Banstead and Epsom. Everyone who took part in these activities was welcomed at John's home, and he arranged for a flag to be hoisted on top of his house, "which signal implied his arrival and desire of receiving his friends". When he was absent "for any period, however short, the colours were struck; by this means there was no disappointment to the visitors desirous of partaking of his festivities..."[118]

Sadly, John's enjoyment of life at his country mansion ended on 19th July, 1788, when he died at Woodcote Lodge at the age of sixty-nine. He was buried in the St. Nicholas Chantry of Croydon Church, where his family placed a marble ledger memorial to him in the Chantry's floor.[119,][120] It seems strange that he chose Croydon for his burial after his long association with Carshalton and its affairs.

John left his goods, chattels, personal estate and effects, the freehold and leasehold properties and lands in Surrey, and £12,000, to young John Hodsdon Durand. He gave Matthew the perpetual advowson, rectory, church and living of Bredon in Worcestershire, and an investment of £12,000 to provide for him until he reached the age of twenty-five, or married, when it would be transferred to him. Each of John's five daughters received £10,000, invested to give them very adequate incomes, and they were encouraged to marry by equal shares in another £10,000, which they became entitled to on their marriages before their respective ages of forty-five, and if the trustees of his will approved of their prospective husbands.[110]

John Durand junior was not treated so kindly by his father, because he already owed him upon bond the sum of £23,256.3s.6d by 1785. Therefore, he was forgiven £12,000 out of the total amount, and received the dividends of £20 per annum share or interest in the long annuities for 1778, but only for his lifetime. Also, young John Hodsdon Durand was given instructions to invest £500 for a Miss Martha Hassell, to provide for her education and maintenance until she was twenty-one, or married, when he could transfer the funds and annuities to her at his discretion. In the meantime, he was asked to give her his "Patronage and Protection". In 1785, Miss Hassell resided at a school in Croydon run by Mrs. Prebble, but her benefactor's will gave no indication of what connection he had with her.[110] He did not hesitate to acknowledge his own children; therefore it was unlikely that she was his daughter, but could have been the illegitimate child of a Mary Hassell, who registered her birth at Beddington in 1772.[121] A likely relative of young Martha, John Hassell, a 'Victualler' of Carshalton, took part in parish affairs when Mr. Durand's involvement with them began,[109] and, perhaps due to their friendship, John senior became Martha's guardian.

The mothers of John's children were not forgotten, although, except for one lady, he did not specifically name them as such persons. These ladies were Elizabeth, the wife of Richard Pearce, a farmer at Ewell; Jane, the wife of Richard Hall, a husbandman of Beddington; Jane, the wife of Richard Divall, who had been Mr. Durand's huntsman, and resided at Walton in Surrey; and, lastly, Elizabeth Stacey of Ewell, who was described as "a singlewoman and the mother of my natural and reputed daughter, Charlotte Durand". They all received a life annuity only, from respective sums of £20 invested in the long annuities for 1778.[110]

John's other bequests included £300 for distribution among the poor of the Hospital for French Protestants in Old Street, London; £100 for the poor of Trinity House Corporation; and all menial servants in his employment at the time of his death were given one year's wages over and above what was due to them. His coachman, William Taylor, had £100, and £10 was left to a Mrs. Naseer of Calcutta, who had been his housekeeper in Bengal (perhaps she was the mother of his eldest son?). In fact, the total legacies in money alone amounted to over £100,000![110]

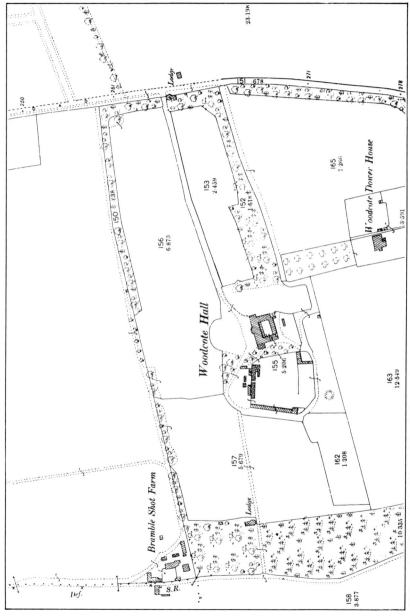

32 A section of the 1896 edition of the Ordnance Survey map showing Woodcote Hall, the east and west lodges and Bramble Shott Farm.

94

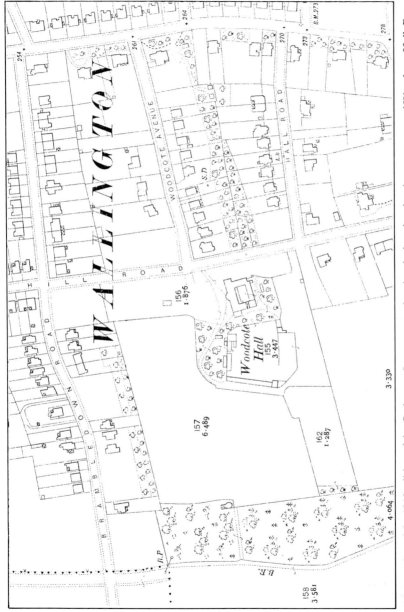

33 A section of the 1913 edition of the Ordnance Survey map, showing the housing developments around Woodcote Hall. By then, the east drive and lodge, and Bramble Shott Farm had all disappeared.

CHAPTER 8

ANOTHER SPORTING GENTLEMAN

Not content with the largest share of his father's estates, John Hodsdon Durand ensured that Miss Hassell's money definitely came under his jurisdiction! Ten days after Mr. Durand senior's will was proved on 31st July, 1788,[110] and with seemingly indecent haste, the banns for John and Martha's marriage were put up in Beddington Church on 10th August! The ceremony took place on 25th August in the presence of the Misses Elizabeth and Sarah Durand, Captain Thomas Brown and Edward Parry,[121] who were two of the trustees of Mr. Durand senior's will, as well as his clerk, Samuel Maddock.[110] If Martha was born in 1772, then she was sixteen years old when she became Mrs. Durand.

The newly-weds resided at Woodcote Lodge, and, in the following year, their son and heir, John Hassell Durand, was born on 6th April, 1789. He was followed by four more children in fairly quick succession, and these were Martha Ann on 18th September, 1790; Elizabeth on 18th September, 1791; James on 6th September, 1793; and George Bartlett on 1st October, 1794; and all of them were baptised on 18th May, 1795.[78, 121] Little George did not live to celebrate his second birthday, and his brother, Charles, whose birth was in 1797, survived only for a few weeks before he, too, died. After him came Caroline[122] and Margaret, and the youngest girl lived until she was fourteen.[117]

Meanwhile, young John had ended his career at sea, and was employed by the East India Company in London.[85] On 11th April, 1789, more lands were added to Little Woodcote when he bought some property which had belonged to James Scawen's mortgaged estate.[70] In the same year, he requested Robert Mylne to design a new house at Woodcote, and, on 24th July, he received three plans, two elevations and a section for it, but the work never commenced. Mr. Mylne was involved with another of John's houses, which he had purchased in Carshalton, and they met on site on 7th October and 12th December, 1789, when the price for the "brick and plaister" work was agreed at £192.2s.5d.[114]

The lease of Bornheim House passed to John on his father's death,[85] and by early 1790, he and Mr. Byne were in dispute over repairs to be carried out on the property. On 25th February, Robert Mylne dined with a Mr. Scott to discuss the problem, and they decided to appoint a Mr. Norris as an "Umpire" in the matter! On 17th April, he met Messrs. Norris and Scott at Carshalton, and took a survey of the "Delapidations of Mr. Byne's house", but no agreement was reached about the work either on that day, or at their other meetings on 22nd and 29th April. Probably, the affair had been settled when Mr. Mylne next visited there, because it was not mentioned again![114]

Preparations were now in hand for alterations to Woodcote Lodge, for which Robert Mylne drew up a plan on 27th May, 1790, although it was not accepted. He returned there on 19th June, and "...set out foundation work etc. of additions to the house, offices etc.", and saw the workmen's progress on site on 24th July.[114] The front of the mansion was extended outwards, with a further extension on the eastern end of it to provide equal proportions on either side of the new main entrance,[36] (see diagram 1) where a portico supported by pillars covered the steps up to double front doors into a large hallway, and behind this was a smaller hall, with a wrought-iron, spiral staircase up to the first floor and an attic above it. Ceiling levels were altered to provide more height to the main rooms, and, after the construction of a lower-pitched roof, most of the attics in the old top storey disappeared, except for the centre portion, which had a small, decorative, round window in the centre gable.[123] The exterior design was typical of the simple, classic style of Mr. Mylne's smaller country houses, such as Addington Lodge at Croydon. Among the advantages gained by employing him were the facts that he conferred with Papworth of London about his stucco and plaster work, the Scottish Ironfounders supplied his grates and stoves, and he was in a position to select marble fireplaces direct from the London firms, who employed Italian carvers. Thus, his ornamental furnishings conformed to those designed by Robert Adam and James Wyatt.[114]

The stabling at the rear of the courtyard at Woodcote Lodge was rebuilt to another of Mylne's designs, and the exterior walls of the house and stables were covered with stucco.[124] The unusual damp-course system here, with its containers for collection of rainwater, also must be attributed to his expertise, as well as the alterations to the outbuildings on the western side of the walled gardens, which included the addition of a first floor at the south-western corner of them to provide accommodation for the estate's bailiff or head gardener. Although this small house has been altered since the late eighteenth century,[49] probably, the original windows here were of a gothic design much favoured by Mr. Mylne.

The octagonal portions added to the small, rectangular gatehouses, East and West Lodges, at the two entrances to the park around Woodcote Lodge, must also be attributed to Robert Mylne. Each addition provided three extra rooms with a shared, central chimney, and bulls-eye windows on six sides of the octagon, while the seventh contained a gothic doorway facing onto the gateway,[65] (see diagram 7).

The best local example of Robert Mylne's penchant for the gothic style can be seen today at 2, Little Woodcote Cottages (part of the old farmhouse). On 28th August, 1790, Mr. Mylne went to Woodcote to discuss the design and building of the farm with Mr. Durand, who had chosen its site on the apex of land where two highways met (Little Woodcote Lane and Woodmansterne Lane). On 13th November, 1790, Mr. Mylne inspected the progress of work both here and at Woodcote Lodge, and gave John "...advice on a Windmill proposition",[114] which could explain the "Mill Bank Field" shown on the map of 1818.[125] Meanwhile, John's appearance at the manorial Court of Carshalton on 25th October in that year, made him the customary tenant of the Greyhound Inn, for which he paid a heriot of a chestnut filly worth £30.[56]

Work on Woodcote Lodge and the farmhouse continued throughout 1791, and Mr. Mylne inspected the builder's progress on 9th April. Apparently, some difficulties arose over the windows installed, because he attended a trial at Croydon on 22nd, 24th and 31st August, 1791, to give testimony on Mr. Durand's behalf about "glass lights, etc.", and met Edward Parry (one of the trustees of John senior's will) at Woodcote on 22nd August. Also, they talked the matter over in a chaise outside the court on 24th August, before Mr. Mylne's evidence was given to a Mr. Pigot at the end of that month.[114]

In January, 1792, John added to Little Woodcote, when he bought some land from Sir John Stanley, and leased ten acres of Clayton (or Claydon) Hill in Wallington from him for a term of five hundred years.[70] The work on Woodcote Lodge and the farmhouse was completed by 7th April, and Mr. Mylne called to inspect it and "settle bills".[114]

The Little Woodcote Farmhouse was then larger than its present-day size (see diagram 8) and the farmer and his family had at least four rooms on the ground floor, with an equal number of bedrooms above. The front door gave access into a small hall with the main staircase, behind which were the bakery and dairy.[126] Probably, accommodation for the domestic and farm servants was on the first floor of the rear, north-eastern section of the building, because there were no attics over the farmer's quarters.[127] A flint wall surrounded the house, and there was a pond in the front garden. The farm's water supply was a well in the farmyard on the opposite side of the lane (Woodmansterne Lane) where there were barns and other buildings.[126] A "Smith's Shop" stood at the rear of the gardens by the other lane[125] (Little Woodcote Lane) so that a blacksmith could be employed to make and repair farm implements and tend to the estate's horses, as well as for the other skills of his trade.

Also in 1792, John bought Carshalton House from Theodore Broadhead[74] and thus became the owner of two important houses in the neighbourhood. His ownership of both properties gave rise to another local legend, which alleged that these were connected to each other by an underground passageway! He retained the lease on Mr. Byne's Bornheim House until after 1801,[85] possibly for the use of his three sisters, Anne, Elizabeth and Sarah, but a Mr. Atkinson became the tenant in 1796.[71] Jane Durand's marriage to Henry Harben of Seaford in Sussex had taken place on 30th September, 1790, in the presence of two of her guardians, Captain Thomas Brown and Edward Parry. Charlotte married Mr. Pellatt Pope of Beddington on 16th July, 1792, with John Hodsdon Durand and William Pellatt as her witnesses,[121] and the bridegroom's name suggests that he was one of Mr. Pellatt's relatives. Both ceremonies took place at Beddington Church.

John became Sheriff of Surrey in 1793,[128] but did not seek a seat in Parliament at that time. He inherited a love of sporting activities from his father, and, probably, was already on friendly terms with his neighbour, the twelfth Earl of Derby, before Mr. Durand senior's death. Two of his horses were entered for the famous race on the Downs, but his colt by Saltram was among the also rans in the Derby on 21st May, 1795, when the entry fee was £1,470; and his Sheet Anchor did not win on 14th May, 1798, after he had paid £1,233.15s.0d. for the horse to run![67] However, he collected some gold and silver cups at race meetings elsewhere, and his Guildford won a silver cup at the Oxford races, while Master Jackey did the same for him at Ascot.[122] His stallions made money for him from stud fees, and Guildford's colt, owned by a Mr. Warrington, was an also ran in the Derby of 1804.[67]

Each year, coursing meetings were held in the countryside between Woodcote and Banstead in February, March, October and November. John had taken over his father's "coursing establishment" at Carshalton, which was "the scene of lively interest", and he became "the very lifespring of the field-sports in the neighbourhood".[118] He supported

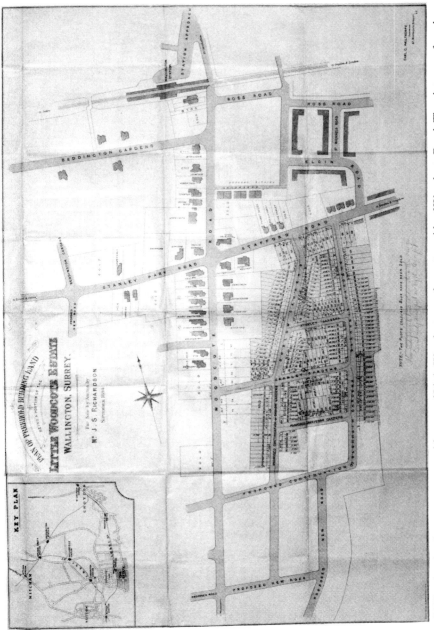

34 Housing developments proposed for part of Little Woodcote, on the eastern side of Woodcote Road. The plots were for sale by auction by Mr. J.S. Richardson in September, 1894.

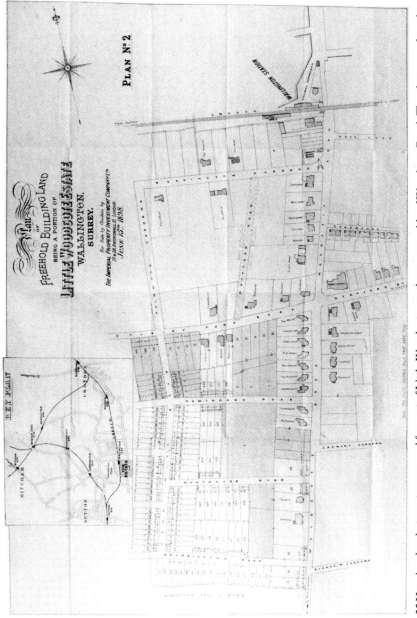

35 Housing developments proposed for part of Little Woodcote, on the western side of Woodcote Road. The plots were for sale by auction by the Imperial Property Investment Company Limited in June, 1898.

Carshalton's cricket team, who had their headquarters at the Greyhound, and, in 1796, he donated a ceramic bowl to them, which he had ordered from the famous Wedgwood Potteries in 1794, and paid £3.10s.0d. by cash for it on 9th January, 1795.[129]

The cricketers kept the bowl with their other goods and chattels at the Greyhound, but after they fell into arrears with payments to the landlady, she seized their belongings in lieu of the money owing to her. Afterwards, she passed on the bowl to her relative, a "Mr. Waite", the Parish Clerk, and, in the late nineteenth century, it was owned by Dr. Barrett of Carshalton House. It was sold in 1909 at Sotheby, Wilkinson and Hodge of London, and, in the details supplied with it at the sale, it was described as one of only two ceramic representations of cricket played with six stumps in the eighteenth century,[78, 88] because usually there were only two stumps with a hole between them at each wicket.[12] This interior medallion also included the initials "J.D." and the year 1796, while the bowl's exterior was decorated with three groups of flowers and fruit.[88]

A Mr. Piers purchased the bowl at the auction, and, afterwards, his appeal for subscribers to this payment met with a good response. The bowl's presentation to Carshalton Urban District Council took place on 9th March, 1910, with the intention that it "should form a nucleus of a museum of such interesting souvenirs..."[130] In 1965, it passed to the London Borough of Sutton, and is now kept in the Central Library's stores, awaiting a borough museum. Over the years, it became known as the "Carshalton Cricket Bowl", although its probable original use was as part of the cricketers' tableware, and not as a prize. Today, it has great value as a rare example of Wedgwood pottery, but, also, it is an important memento of young Mr. Durand, the owner of Woodcote Lodge and Little Woodcote in the late eighteenth and early nineteenth centuries.

John sold "Carshalton House" to Mr. David Mitchell in 1799,[74] and, at about this time, he acquired a house in Green Street, Grosvenor Square,[117] in the most fashionable part of Georgian London, which was nearer to the Earl of Derby's town-house than the late Mr. Durand's property in Hinde Street. He attained his "symbol of success" and entered Parliament, when he obtained the seat for Maidstone in Kent at the election in June, 1802. The only available details of his political career are reports in old newspapers about his campaign, in which he "suddenly appeared out of the blue and won"![131] Probably, his success was due to his ability to offer the largest sums of money to the most influential voters there! Consequently, when Manning and Bray published the first volume of their work on Surrey, in 1804, John Hodsdon Durand, M.P., was included in their list of subscribers.[11]

At the next election, in 1806, John did not campaign for another seat in the Commons. His sporting activities had increased after the Earl of Derby decided to keep a pack of stag hounds at the Oaks, and brought his own stags from his family seat, Knowsley in Lancashire,[132] to his deer paddock adjoining the lane to Woodmansterne.[133] John's tribute to his happy hunting days with Lord Derby and the hounds was a wooden tower, with a staircase inside it leading up to a large metal and gilt stag on the top of it. This "monument" stood on part of the ancient enclosure at the end of Oak Stubbs Shott, by Milton Hill, so that the Earl could see it from the windows of his mansion. The land here was called "Stag Field" until the beginning of the present century, although the tower was taken down long before then.[82, 134]

Sheepfarming still took place on the downlands around Woodcote Lodge, but the sheepwalk belonging to the house had disappeared, probably in the division of Woodcote into Greater and Little. John owned flocks of sheep and leased another sheepwalk leading from Banstead, along the north side of Long Gallop (approximately by the present-day Pine Walk) down onto the highway (Woodmansterne Road) towards Little Woodcote,[125] and belonging to Carshalton's lord of the manor, George Taylor, who also rented some of Mr. Durand's land.[89] The total parish rates for the whole of John's estate, including his leasehold lands, came to £675.2s.0d. per annum (£409.5s.0d. to Carshalton, and the reduced annual value of £265.17s.0d. to Beddington).[89, 135]

From the early nineteenth century onwards, another local legend about Woodcote Lodge's secret underground passage alleged that it connected the mansion with the caves at Beddington. It has been suggested that these were constructed or enlarged as a place where smugglers could hide their contraband, which was carried here at night by trains of donkeys along the old bridleway across the downs from Reigate.[59] Therefore, the story could suggest that John was one of the rich patrons of this clandestine "sport", and, maybe, some fine wines and spirits were quietly delivered to his home adjacent to this highway! Unfortunately, the justification for this tale has been lost over the years. (The caves are probably natural in origin, but worked on by man for various purposes at various times.)

By about 1809, John and Martha had separated after a breakdown in their marriage, and, perhaps, Mrs. Durand had found other diversions to tempt her away from her husband. Their second son, James, probably supported his mother's cause, because he gained his father's displeasure![122] Their youngest daughter, Margaret, lived with her mother at Green Street, Grosvenor Square,[117] but the other girls, Martha Ann, Elizabeth and Caroline, remained faithful to him for the remainder of his life.[122]

His wife's desertion was a bitter blow for John. He lost interest in farming his lands and, from 1809 until 1816, leased most of his estate to tenant farmers, while he gave up his own leases from other landowners; but, in 1817, he became Mr. Byne's tenant once again.[89] He withdrew from his sporting activities and lived the life of a recluse at Woodcote Lodge,[118] although he still owned a sailing yacht,[122] and could outclass the keen "four-in-hand" drivers of that period by handling a "coach-and-six".[88] His eldest son, John Hassell Durand, resided with him at the mansion, and Miss Clara Warren was employed as their housekeeper. She proved to be very successful in her work, so that both of them grew very fond of her, and, eventually, their appreciation for the way in which she cared for them was shown in their wills.[122, 136]

During this period, John lost two members of his family. There was a monument in Croydon churchyard to an "Anna Durand", whose death occurred on 28th June, 1812, at the age of sixty-one years,[119] who, probably, was his eldest sister, Anne. In late January, 1814, his youngest daughter, Margaret, died at the house in Green Street, Grosvenor Square, and was buried at Carshalton on 1st February.[117] Perhaps, as a result of this last unhappy event, young John Hassell Durand made out a new will on 25th August in the same year, when he was twenty-five years old. He had drawn up several wills previously,[136] which suggests that, as well as being a wealthy young man, he did not enjoy good health.

In 1818, John decided to sell Woodcote Lodge and Little Woodcote, and reinvest his money in bank stocks and securities. Possibly, by then, he realised that he did not need to keep his mansion and its estate for his eldest son to inherit, because of his ill-health, and he did not intend to leave these for James. After completion of the sale in September, 1818,[56] the two John Durands and their housekeeper, Miss Warren, moved to a house somewhere in Sutton.[122]

John had some more legal matters to finalise in 1819, because his father's goods, chattels and credits had not been administered according to his will by his executors, Captain Thomas Brown, Edward Parry, the Reverend John Smith and Commander John Bartlett. Furthermore,

Home Farm Dairy

Fresh Butter
New Laid Eggs
Milk & Cream

LAYING TRAMWAY LINES.
STAFFORD ROAD, WALLINGTON. July 1906.

From the E. Y. Photo.
Wallington

36 Laying the tramway lines in Stafford Road, Wallington, in July, 1906. The dairy in the background stood on the corner of Elgin Road.

Captain Brown, the Reverend Mr. Smith and Mr. Parry had died; therefore, after Commander Bartlett renounced the probate, John was sworn as the administrator and residuary legatee of Mr. Durand senior's estates on 23rd March, 1819.[110] About three weeks later, he sold the Greyhound Inn at Carshalton to Daniel Tarling, who paid £1,650 for it on 14th April, when he was admitted as the customary tenant at the manorial Court of Carshalton.[56]

Young John Hassell Durand lived to the age of thirty-one years, and after his death at the end of December, 1820, he was buried in Carshalton churchyard on 2nd January, 1821.[117] He gave £10,000 to his "honoured father", and left £5,000 for an investment to provide an income for the sole use of his "dear sister Caroline". Miss Warren received an annuity from £2,000 invested on her behalf, and another £1,000 was used for the same purpose for a Miss Mary Ann Clives. His two friends, Robert Oliver, gentleman, and Joseph King, a solicitor of Bedford Row, were his trustees and executors, and each of them had £100 as a token of his esteem for them; also, Mr. King was given the remainder of his possessions.[136] It would be difficult to assess his relationship with Miss Clives. Perhaps, he had hoped to marry her, or she had been employed as a governess, or nurse, in previous years. Similar to Miss Warren, she was rewarded for her devotion to him by receipt of a substantial income for her lifetime.

By 1827, John and Clara Warren had moved from Sutton to the village of Kennington, where Caroline lived with her husband, William Matthews, who was a stockbroker. John's eldest girl, Martha Ann, had married Thomas Deacon, and they resided in the "East Indies", and Elizabeth was the wife of John Goodall. Miss Warren's death in 1828 must have been another great loss to John, who had become very ill by then. Consequently, Miss Charlotte Maria Hart was employed in her place to look after him, because he needed constant care and attention. His friend and surgeon, Dr. Edward Wallace of Carshalton, attended him during his illness.[122]

In about the second week of January, 1830, John, his daughter, Caroline, and her husband, together with Miss Hart and his nurse, Mrs. Mary Weight, the wife of George Weight of Carshalton, went to the Greyhound Inn at Sutton, where they stayed for a few weeks. When John's doctor, Edward Wallace, called to see him there on 4th February, his patient informed him that he would like a confidential discussion about a reward for Miss Hart, because of the competent way in which she had looked after him. Mr. and Mrs. Matthews, and Mrs. Weight, were asked to leave the room, and, when they were alone, John agreed with Dr. Wallace on an annuity of £50 for his housekeeper after his death. John Grace senior was called to witness a codicil to Mr. Durand's will and his signature of a cross made with the doctor's help.[122]

John died at the end of February, 1830, at the age of sixty-eight years, and was buried in Carshalton churchyard on 8th March.[117] Before his will of 18th March, 1827, and the codicil dated 4th February, 1830, could be proved, Dr. Wallace, Mrs. Weight and Mr. Grace senior appeared at court on 27th March to swear on oath that the latter document was made out and signed as required by law, and that Mr. Durand was of sound, rational mind at the time, although bodily disabled and had required assistance to make his mark. These facts were confirmed on oath by Caroline and William Matthews on 29th March, and both documents were proved on 3rd April, 1830.[122]

In John's will, he left Martha Ann and Elizabeth an annuity of £400 each, while Caroline had one of £250. All of the girls' incomes increased after the sale of his gold cups, sailing yacht and other effects, his real estate, the residue of his stocks, funds, monies, mortgages, securities for money, goods, chattels and personal estate. James Durand only received £100 per annum for life, until he tried to mortgage, encumber or dispose of the payment before receipt of it, and on his death, the annuity reverted back into his father's personal estate. Mrs. Martha Durand lost her income from an investment made for that purpose after she deserted her husband. However, she was not left destitute, because £500 was bequeathed to her,[122] which was the sum John had been instructed to invest for her under the terms of his father's will![110]

If Miss Warren had survived him, she would have been amply rewarded for her devotion to John by receipt of an income from another investment of £6,666.13s.4d. in Bank of England annuities, and one quarter of this amount was due to be transferred to her absolutely for her to leave to her appointed heir in her own will, if she had not received the money during her lifetime. John's silver tea-urn made from the cup won by his horse, "Guildford", at the Oxford races was bequeathed to her, as well as a silver tankard which she had presented to her employer during her many years of service with him.[122]

The executors of John's will, Dr. Edward Wallace, Jonas William Powell of West Rudham in Norfolk, and John Roots, a yeoman of Cotesford in Oxford, each received £200 as a token of his respect and regard for them, and for the execution of the trusts. Probably, the last two gentlemen were involved with his horse-racing enterprises, and, if

Mr. Roots had not predeceased Mr. Durand, he was due to receive the silver cup won at Ascot by "Master Jackey", which suggests that he had trained this horse. The respective sums of £100 were left to the trustees of Christ's Hospital and to the trustees of the Bridewell and Bethelan (Bethlehem) Hospitals for use in these institutions, and every servant employed by John at the time of his death had £10 for mourning, except for Miss Hart, who received her annuity of £50.[122] It seems likely that his nurse, Mrs. Weight, also requested her husband to obtain the cricket bowl from his relative at the Greyhound in Carshalton, to provide her with a keepsake in memory of her late employer.

Another John Durand appears in the Carshalton Parish Registers. He was born in 1779, and after his death at the age of fifty-five, he was buried in Carshalton churchyard on 14th September, 1834.[117] He did not leave a will[137] from which his identity could have been established, but, perhaps, he was John Hodsdon Durand's nephew, and the son of his eldest brother, John.

37 Woodcote Road, Wallington, near Woodcote Green. The road on the left is Marchmont Road. The entrance to Dower Avenue is at the end of the line of trees on the right-hand side. (see section of the 1913 edition of the Ordnance Survey map on p.95.)

CHAPTER 9

CHANGES AT WOODCOTE

While Mr. Durand lived quietly at Sutton and Kennington, the new owner of Woodcote Lodge and Little Woodcote, William Turner, enjoyed the last eleven years of his life there as a country gentleman. The estate's sale was completed on 24th September, 1818, when he was admitted as the customary tenant of the copyhold land in Long Furlong,[56] so that, altogether, he had acquired a total of just over six hundred and forty-eight acres mostly comprising large, arable fields, with sixty acres of pasture for sheep, cattle and horses.[125] At some time before 1829, he purchased other parts of Wall Shott, Bowling Green Shott, Holloway Shott and No Man's Land, and called the new fields East and West Shotts.[138] The northern boundary of the largest section of his estate then extended as far as the site of the present-day railway line.

William Turner came from the village of West Ham where he had another estate,[138] and, near there, a Mr. Turner's sailcloth warehouse stood in Limehouse adjacent to the East India Docks on the Thames.[139, 140] If this establishment belonged to him, he and the Durands had mutual interests in the merchant fleet, but, unlike them, he only had one child. His daughter, Mary Ann, had been married for some years before he arrived at Woodcote Lodge, and he disapproved of her husband, William Stephens Meryweather, because he failed to provide her with a permanent home! However, their marriage provided him with six grandchildren, all of whom met with his approval![141]

Although he did not gain a notoriety for his sporting activities, Mr. Turner's name appeared in the list of owners for horses which 'also ran' in the Derby on Thursday, 19th May, 1823, when he paid £1,863.15s.0d. for his colt by "Phantom" to enter the race.[67] There were plenty of opportunities for him to go hunting with his neighbours when he came to Woodcote. Apart from the Earl of Derby at The Oaks, Mrs. Anne Paston Gee, then a widow, had inherited the Carew estates on the death of her brother-in-law, Richard Gee Carew, in 1816,[26] and she joined the hunts with her harriers and kept her deer in a paddock at Beddington Park; also there was Mr. Taylor's herd at Carshalton.[78, 142]

From the late 1820s onwards, changes began to take place not only among the ageing local sporting people, but also at Woodcote. In 1828, Greater Woodcote passed to a new owner when Mrs. Gee died and left her estates to her cousin, Sir Benjamin Hallowell, who took the surname and arms of Carew. He was an Admiral of Canadian origins, who had served under Nelson's command at the Battle of the Nile, and received his knighthood in 1815.[26] At Little Woodcote, William Turner was already a widower by the time of his death on 19th September, 1829.[141] Afterwards, Woodcote Lodge and its estate were never owned again by one person, and were either under joint ownership, or the property of successive companies.[138]

William's real and personal estates at West Ham and Little Woodcote were left to four trustees, who were his brother, John Turner; his two nephews, John Hornblow Turner and William Binns Wood; and his friend, William Taylor Abud. He gave £500 to his daughter, Mary Ann, and recommended her to use it "in furnishing a House for her own use"! His household goods, furniture, books, wines, liquors, carriages, horses, and other "moveable effects", were sold, and the proceeds, together with any debts owing to him, his Bank of England investments, and annual incomes from his freehold, copyhold and leasehold properties, were invested to provide an annuity for Mary Ann of £500, which increased to £1,000 on her husband's death, and further annuities of £300 for her eldest son, William Turner Meryweather, £200 for the eldest girl, another Mary Ann, and £150 each for the four other children, Maria Frances, Montague John, Marcus William and Matilda Sarah, who was known as Maud. Respective sums of money were left to his sister-in-law, Miss Elizabeth Ethersey, his sister, Rebecca Wood, another brother, Joseph Turner, Mrs. Henry Turner, a Miss Hornblow, Mrs. Thomlinson, and Mr. Richard Abud, as well as to his trustees, and John Hornblow Turner received all of his dogs.[141]

The servants at Woodcote Lodge were not forgotten, and Martha Mortlock, who, probably, was his housekeeper, was given £40; the coachman, Joseph Anderson, had £10, and so did the footman and gardener, while the groom and female servants received £5 each. Lastly, the plate and linen were divided between William's eldest grandson and granddaughter, William and Mary Ann, as and when they became twenty-one years of age. His trustees were appointed as guardians of each grandchild, and were wholly responsible for their education and maintenance, without their parents' interference, because of their doubtful ability to rear them in the correct manner! They became entitled to incomes from their grandfather's estates at the age of twenty-five, but each grandson had to qualify for his income by obtaining "His Majesty's Royal License and Authority" to take and use the surname and arms of Turner within twelve months of their twenty-first birthdays, otherwise the monies were forfeited![141]

After William's will had been proved on 3rd December, 1829,[141] the four trustees took over the administration of his estates, and were admitted as the customary tenants of the copyhold lands in Long Furlong on 15th April, 1830.[56] In the following years, both Woodcote Lodge and Little Woodcote were leased to tenants until most of the grandchildren reached the age of twenty-five, when they received their respective incomes from the properties.[141] Marcus and Montague Meryweather took the surname and arms of Turner on 26th November, 1830,[138] and their eldest brother, William, had already done so by then.

Two more changes took place in the neighbourhood in 1834. The twelfth Earl of Derby, who was now over eighty years old, decided to sell his sporting seat in 1833,[143] and Sir Charles Edward Grey bought The Oaks from him in February, 1834.[144] In the same year, Greater Woodcote also had a new owner after Sir Benjamin Hallowell Carew's death, when he was succeeded by his son, Charles Hallowell Carew.[26]

In his booklet, *The Parish of Beddington in the year 1837*, Mr. Ron Michell described Woodcote Lodge at that time as: "...standing in its own park to the south of Wallington's common fields. The principal well of this house was deep with a large shed built over it. It had two large buckets feeding into a storage tank, a donkey walked round harnessed to a long pole and, as one bucket went down, the other came up. A hook was put from the tank to an iron rail around the bucket, and, as the donkey continued to pull, the water was tipped into a storage tank. The animal was then turned the other way round to bring up the second bucket. There was a second well at the side of the mansion."

One of the successful, wealthy, local farmers, Thomas Weall, had become the tenant of Woodcote Lodge and Little Woodcote by 1839.[145] He and his wife, Margaret, lived at the mansion with their six children, and were able to afford four female and two male servants to look after their household.[146] Mr. Weall's father, Thomas Weall senior, had farmed lands in Greater Woodcote for many years, and was the rated occupier of about eight hundred acres and the Woodcote Farm there,[147] whereas he had rented forty-one acres of the Old Lodge from Richard Gee Carew in 1806.[135]

As well as his farmlands in Carshalton, Mr. Weall junior used two

38 Front entrance to Stanley house. Note the wrought-ironwork on the portico, and the wide eaves with modillions on the roof.

hundred and eleven acres of Little Woodcote in Beddington's parish for pasture, fir plantations, arable land and an orchard.[147] Probably, he supervised the people at the Little Woodcote Farm, because there was no farmer in residence at that time, only four agricultural labourers; the shepherd, Samuel Pearce; and Edward Lane, the gamekeeper.[146]

The branch line of the London, Brighton and South Coast Railway, part of which ran along the northern boundary of Little Woodcote's largest section, was opened in 1844, and brought great changes to the surrounding countryside in the latter half of the nineteenth century. The opening ceremony of Wallington's railway station took place in 1847, but this was named "Carshalton", because the railway company had been unable to purchase any land nearer to the larger of the two villages.[15]

The eldest of William Turner's grandchildren, William, died in May, 1841, and the income from his share of the estates was divided between his brothers and sisters.[138] By 1851, Mr. Weall and his family had left Woodcote Lodge, and Montague Turner, with the Misses Maria and Maud Meryweather, had taken up residence there. Montague was thirty-nine years old, a captain in the militia, and considered himself as one of the landed gentry; while Maria was twenty-nine, and Maud twenty-four. They were looked after by their housekeeper, Mrs. Maddock; a ladies' maid; one housemaid, a footman and a footboy. Two gardeners were employed to tend the grounds around the mansion, and the coachman, William Longhurst, lived above the coach-house with his family.[148]

A tenant farmer, John Woolhead, had taken over four hundred and seventy acres of Little Woodcote, and lived at the farmhouse with his wife, Lucilla, their five children, three farm servants, and two house-servants. The gamekeeper, Mr. Lane, had left, but Samuel Pearce, the shepherd, was still employed although he was seventy-three years old – there was no retirement pension in those days! The other four agricultural workers and their families were housed in some tenements.[148]

The Commons Enclosure Award of 1853 brought some changes to Little Woodcote. With the exception of approximately nine acres of copyhold land in Long Furlong, and including about two hundred and five arable acres in Carshalton, it became a freehold estate held by William Turner's surviving trustees, who were his two nephews, J.H. Turner and W.B. Wood.[138] At that time they were in dispute with Carshalton's lord of the manor, Mr. Taylor, about the ownership of some property in the parish[78] – perhaps Daniel Burrell's survey map had been mislaid? The Award abolished a few of the old highways used for many years. The road between Milton Hill and Long Furlong was "stopped up", as well as one bounded by Vicars Cross and Sand Piece Shotts leading southwards to Little Woodcote Farm. New roads appeared, such as Park Lane at the northern end of the Bridle Way (Boundary Road), and "New Road" (Stanley Park Road).[78]

The Carews' long association with Woodcote ended in 1859, although, for about forty-three years, their estates had been held by people of that name but not related to the family. Charles Hallowell Carew died in 1847, and his son, Charles Hallowell Hallowell Carew, was considerably indebted to money-lenders by then. He held on to his properties until 1859, when he was obliged to sell them to pay off his debts amounting to £350,000! His manors of Beddington and Norbury were divided into lots and sold by auction, so that the lands passed to many new owners.[26]

In the same year, a new method of farming began at Little Woodcote when James Arnot, now the tenant farmer of four hundred acres there, purchased a Fowler's steam-plough for his arable fields, and used it for hire on his neighbours' lands. He, his wife and family, lived at the farmhouse with their servants. In July, 1861, he entered a prolonged trial of steam-ploughing, held by the Royal Agricultural Society of England at Leeds. The competition was between farmers using his type of plough and those with the Howard's modification known as the "Smith's system". The trials favourably impressed the editor of the *Agricultural Gazette*, Mr. J.C. Norton, who was among the spectators. During the following months, he inspected the competitors' farms, including Mr. Arnot's, and discussed the merits of these machines. Afterwards, his condensed reports of the interviews were included in his *New Farmer's Almanac* for 1862, in which he described Little Woodcote's farmlands as: "...a tract of open countryside and light calcareous soil of various depth – upon the chalk about a mile from the Carshalton Station on the London and Epsom Railway..."[149]

In his discussion with Mr. Norton, Mr. Arnot told him that he had owned his Fowler's steam-plough since the harvest of 1859, and worked a three-furrow plough. He paid £700 for the machine, including the rope and engine, and had ploughed three hundred and three acres in 1859-60, and three hundred and eighty-nine in 1860-61, at the rate of six or seven acres per day for ordinary ploughing, or three acres for the ten and twelve inch-deep work (one acre per furrow). He completed the whole area in eighty days at an average of five acres daily, and one hundred and fifty for his neighbours at twelve shillings per acre. The engine was used for threshing purposes on two hundred and twenty acres of his own land, as well as two hundred and fifty elsewhere for hire. The annual estimated costs amounted to £222 inclusive of repairs, labour, fuel, horse and water cart, and depreciation; but, after deducting the yearly profits gained by hired steam-ploughing for at least forty days, the sum did not exceed £190, or ten shillings and sixpence per acre, so that £150 (or seven shillings and sixpence per acre) appeared to be the correct estimate per annum.[149]

In previous years, when the horse-drawn plough was used, thirteen horses were kept on the farm, and each one received two and a half bushels of oats, with the same amount of hay, weekly for seven months of the year. Therefore, he paid £29 per annum per horse, including depreciation of implements and services of the farrier, blacksmith and saddler. Also, the ploughman's wages and his cottage added another £16 onto the cost of each animal, and brought the total to £45. The whole expenditure for the old method of ploughing came to one half more than the money he paid out even on "the highest estimate upon the engine which had displaced them", and nearly double the sum incurred after deduction of profits made on hired work![149] Probably, such an enthusiastic report tempted many farmers to purchase steam-ploughs, which were less expensive to maintain!

The southern end of Little Woodcote retained its rural character throughout the latter half of the nineteenth century and into the twentieth, while the northern part of the estate was slowly transformed by property developments resulting from the easy access by rail to and from London, and the desire of many people there for a home in pleasant surroundings. New roads and houses appeared in Wall Shott, Bowling Green Shott, Holloway and Smoke Shotts, and, after completion of the church in Manor Road in 1867, Wallington became a parish, whereas, previously, it had been included in Beddington.[15]

In the 1860s, another housing development began on Little Woodcote's western edge, and covered the estate's small strips of land in Sandpiece and Vicars Cross Shotts along two new roads formed following the Commons Enclosure Award. Stanley House, with its outbuildings and stables, was one of the first properties in Stanley Road, and was built by William Alfred Gale, who used it as security for various mortgages while it was let to tenants.[150] By 1868, Gale and Alexandra Terraces, and the Stanley Hotel, stood on its southern side. A row of

39 (*above*): Woodcote Hall divided into two houses, c.1920. No. 66 Park Hill Road was on the left-hand side, and the right-hand side was called 'The Old Hall'.
40 (*below*): Woodcote Hall, August, 1987. Restoration work on the house was completed in 1983.

large houses called "Woodcote View" had been erected in The Avenue, and three residences in New Road (Stanley Park Road) had gardens on the site of present-day North and South Avenues. The water supply for all of these dwellings was obtained from draw-wells.[151]

The pleasant surroundings of this new, select neighbourhood known as Carshalton on the Hill, was soon threatened by plans for an intensive housing project drawn up in 1870. Sites for one hundred and nineteen houses were marked on the plan for The Avenue, and fifty-nine of them backed onto Stanley Road. Building plots were leased to various builders for terms of ninety-nine years, and some work commenced in the intended roads on the western side of Stanley Road called Blanche, Edmund, Florence and Violet Streets, while a Florence Road was planned for the line of present-day East and West Cranfield Roads.[150] Fortunately, most of the development never materialised, because of the lack of amenities such as piped water and gas supplies, which were more important to prospective buyers than the attractive scenery!

The tenants of Stanley House in 1871 were John E. Crickner, who worked for the London Stock Exchange, and his sister, Miss M.E.E. Crickner, whose occupation was that of an accountant, and they had a cook and a housemaid to look after them.[152] They had left by 8th June, 1874, when Mr. Gale sold the property to a chartered accountant, William Russell Crowe.[150] He moved there with his wife and young family and one servant, and Captain Crowe and his wife, Mary, lived next-door in the new Stanley Villas. Both Captain and Mr. Crowe took part in the local Conservative Party's activities during the following years.[153, 154]

Miss Maud Meryweather now lived on her own at Woodcote Lodge, after Montague's departure to a house in Kensington and Maria's marriage to a Mr. W.C. Hadden. Both Marcus and Montague had gained some benefits on the death of their father in March, 1863, when their life shares of their grandfather's estates were freed from the trusts of his will. In 1868, the trustees made them tenants-in-common with equal rights to nearly half of Little Woodcote's income, and this led to disputes between them and their two younger sisters,[138] who, probably, felt that they, too, were due for an increase in their own incomes! Their eldest sister, Mary Ann, avoided these arguments. Her social status had improved when she married and became Lady Sandys,[138] and could thus claim that her husband's ancestors held the manor of West Ham in the early part of the eighteenth century.[139]

The quarrels continued throughout 1868 and, finally, ended in the

High Court of Chancery, where judgement was given on 12th January, 1869, in favour of Marcus and Montague, who were made joint owners of Woodcote Lodge and two hundred and thirty-one acres of Little Woodcote in lieu of the income they had received from the trustees in April, 1868! Maria and Maud were ordered to pay the legal costs of the proceedings,[138] and the hostile situation within the family did not improve! The brothers then decided to profit from the property developments in Wallington by leasing and selling some of their lands,[138] and the houses in "Rosemount" had been built by 1871[152] on the site of the present-day shopping precinct known as Wallington Square. They sold more plots on the opposite side of the Hollow Way (Woodcote Road) for other large residences, and leased their land by Wallington Station to tenants for ninety-nine years, at an annual rent of fifteen pounds.[138]

Lady Sandys had become a widow by 1871, and stayed for a while with her sister at Woodcote Lodge. Maud employed a housekeeper and one domestic servant at that time. Probably her housekeeping money was restricted after she paid the costs of her court case, but she managed to afford a gardener, William Walton, to tend the grounds around the mansion, although both East and West Lodges were empty.[152]

James Arnot continued to prosper and now had five hundred acres of farmlands at Little Woodcote. Consequently, forty-one people lived at the farm by 1871! He occupied the farmhouse with his family, an agricultural science student, and two female servants. His employees, including a steam-ploughman, and their families were housed in eight cottages, while a dwelling in the cowshed provided a home for two unmarried women; and two single men had their living quarters in the harness-room![152] Within the next few years, a new farmhouse (the Old Lodge Farm) was built for Mr. Arnot to ease the housing situation, and the old one became two dwellings.[153]

After about twenty-four years at Woodcote Lodge, Miss Maud Meryweather died on 12th March, 1875, at the age of forty-eight, and her share of her grandfather's estates was divided between her brothers and sisters.[138] Marcus and Montague then changed the mansion's name to Woodcote Hall before it was let to Mr. Edward Wormald in 1876. The local people took some time to become accustomed to the fact that a new "Woodcote Lodge" was completed in the same year on the first plot of land on the left-hand side of Woodcote Road from Stafford Road![154]

Mr. Wormald was a wholesale stationer, and took an active part in the affairs of the local Conservative Party.[153, 154] He and his wife, Annette, with their two young daughters, Marjory and Lettice, lived at Woodcote Hall for about another six years. Their domestic staff consisted of a cook, a parlour-maid, two housemaids, a kitchen-maid, the children's nurse, and a groom. They had three gardeners, one of whom lived in the East Lodge with his family; the second was housed in rooms over the "sheds" by the walled gardens, and the third resided at the West Lodge with his mother and his father, who was a cowman. The coachman, his wife, a harness maker, and the former coachman, occupied the stables cottage.[153] The Bramble Shott Farm was built about this time and stood where the present-day Brambledown Road crosses over Boundary Road,[134] and its occupants were a farm labourer, his wife and their young son.[153]

During the first two years of Mr. Wormald's tenancy of Woodcote Hall, it was investigated by a member of the Surrey Archaeological Society. At one of the Society's meetings on 14th March, 1877, Dr. Shorthouse of Carshalton reported that there was a "cavern or something of that kind" in front of the mansion (he used the name of Woodcote Lodge on that occasion) and, as far as he knew, it had not been explored by any archaeologists.[155] Unfortunately, he did not give its exact location, and it has not been traced since then!

One week after Lady Sandys' death on 7th January, 1879, when her share of the estates was divided between her brothers and Maria Hadden, Marcus and Montague used Woodcote Hall and their part of Little Woodcote as security for a mortgage of just over £80,000, although the lands could be sold when required and by amicable agreement. Consequently, the "Dower House" was built in 1880, on a plot in Mill Bank Field purchased by a Mr. Edwyn Jones.[138] By 1881, two farmers had taken over Mr. Arnot's tenancy of Little Woodcote Farm. Mr. Adams farmed one hundred and ten acres assisted by six labourers and a farm servant, and he and his wife occupied the new farmhouse. The other farmer, Moses Miller, looked after fifty acres with four of his five sons – his youngest boy and only daughter were both at school. He and his family lived in one dwelling in the old farmhouse, while the second housed a building labourer, his wife and six children. Three more cottages provided homes for the farm bailiff and Mr. Adams' employees; also two men lived in a shed![153]

Marcus and Montague Turner became entitled to equal shares of the income from their grandfather's estates when Maria Hadden died on 7th February, 1882, without any heirs. The trustees conveyed the remainder of Little Woodcote to them on 1st May, 1882, except for one acre in

Catsbrain Shott, which had been sold, and some of the West Ham properties. They had paid off a considerable amount of their mortgage, but decided to take out another one with a different company in June, 1882, so that the outstanding debt of just over £28,000 could be paid and they had about £58,000 for themselves.[138] Mr. Wormald and his family left Woodcote Hall in the same year, and the house stood empty for a while.[154]

In 1885, Montague Turner returned to Woodcote Hall,[154] but he and his brother, Marcus, did not repay any of the money loaned to them by the agreed date. Legal action against them and the other gentlemen involved in their mortgage, including the trustees of their grandfather's West Ham estates, was heard in the High Court of Justice, Chancery Division, on 20th February, 1886. Judgement was given against them, so that all of them were thenceforth debarred from any rights, title, interest, equity and redemption of the mansion and Little Woodcote, and the Scottish Provident Institution (the Mortgagees) became the new owners of these properties.[138] Afterwards, the Institution began to sell more lands in the estate's northern section for new housing developments to recoup some of their lost finances.

Meanwhile, Carshalton on the Hill had become a popular place for wealthy people to visit for holidays or convalescence, because of its healthy, rural surroundings. The Stanley Hotel had prospered, and was re-organised, so that it provided many comforts for its guests. French and German were spoken there for the convenience of foreign visitors, and the attractions offered included billiards, lawn tennis, cricket, pleasure grounds, good stabling and well-stocked cellars.[154] The hotel's popularity began to decline when part of the proposed intensive housing development for The Avenue commenced with the erection of three large terraces of houses, two of which backed on to the opposite side of Stanley Road. Each dwelling was three storeys high above a basement, and more suitable for an inner suburb of London, where space was limited. The houses were not completed, and became the subject of ridicule by Carshalton's inhabitants, who called the development "Jerusalem", probably resultant from some kind of feud between them and the residents on the hill,[156] and the fact that the project's financier was a Mr. Israel Abraham![150]

Because of the lack of amenities, the new houses in The Avenue failed to attract the wealthier members of Victorian society for whom they were intended. Instead, squatters and their families invaded the empty properties and turned them into flats, but, without proper maintenance,

41 The West Lodge, 1986.

the buildings deteriorated and slowly became slums. Other parts of the development abandoned in the proposed new streets were cleared away and replaced by smaller houses in Stanley Road, and North and South Avenues;[156] also, shops were built on the south side of Stanley Park Road by the beginning of the present century. Despite the change of scenery opposite Stanley House, Mr. Crowe's family lived there until 1906, although his son took over the house in 1896.[154] Before the Stanley Hotel closed in 1897, it gained a dubious reputation as a venue for clandestine weekends enjoyed by certain gentlemen and their "ladies"! It was sold to a temperance society called "The Sons of the Phoenix", who re-named it "Phoenix House", and, paradoxically, the bar-room became their church! The remainder of the building was used as an orphanage for over thirty years.[157]

The Scottish Provident Institution placed Woodcote Hall in the hands of local estate agents, so that it could be let to suitable tenants, but it remained empty for about nine years. In 1888, Police Constable E. Pryer was installed there to ensure that no unwelcome intruders took over the property. From 1895 until 1897, it was occupied by a Major-General Montague Brown,[154] who was the last tenant, probably because it could no longer be classed as a country mansion, owing to the new housing projects in progress on some of its parklands. Also, the land at the rear of the draw-well had been sold for the first St. Patrick's Church, housed in a small corrugated-iron building.[138]

The Imperial Property Development Company Limited had purchased a good deal of land in Bramble Shott and south Bowling Green Shott. Their Woodcote Estate Office stood on the corner of Stanley Park and Woodcote Roads in 1890, until its site was sold, when they moved to larger premises near the railway station.[154] In June, 1898, their clients were informed of a forthcoming auction of freehold lands on 7th September, 1898, at the Greyhound Hotel in Croydon. The plots offered for sale were in their new Brambledown, Park Hill, Heathdene and Hawthorn Roads for "houses of good accommodation...situated on high ground, in the midst of charming walks and drives...", which was "exceptionally dry and healthy..." with easy access to the City and West End on a frequent train service from Wallington.[158]

Some shops stood by the railway station and on the opposite side of Woodcote Road, at the beginning of the present century. In 1906, a new type of transport appeared, after completion of the tram-tracks between Croydon and Sutton within six weeks,[159] providing easy access for both Wallington's and Carshalton's increasing population to larger shopping facilities. Its route passed through the northern part of Little Woodcote, along Stanley Park and Stafford Roads. Except for the commencement of the hospital development in 1903, the estate's southern lands remained in a rural state. Mr. Lobjoit occupied the new farmhouse from 1888 until 1901, while two dwellings in the old house, and three more cottages, housed the farmworkers. In 1889, Bramble Shott Farm had been taken over by the Matthews brothers,[154] who, probably, were descendants of Moses Matthews, a tenant farmer of John Hodsdon Durand and William Turner in previous years.[135, 160] Their tenancy lasted until the farm buildings were demolished in about 1904.[154]

CHAPTER 10

SCENES FROM EARLY SUBURBAN LIFE

Woodcote Hall remained empty during the first years of the present century. Its depleted parklands presented an enticing play area for local children, who had easy access to them through adjacent building sites, and the old mansion was an extra attraction here. Consequently, young Master Allen from Elgin Road in Wallington ventured too near the deep draw-well one day, fell into it and was drowned! After this tragedy, the well was covered over, and caretakers were installed at the house to deter intruders both young and old.[161, 123]

The late Mrs. Patricia Clark, who died in November, 1984, spent part of her childhood at Woodcote Hall, when her step-grandparents, Mr. and Mrs. Parris, were the caretakers. She moved there in 1910, with her father and step-mother, Mr. and Mrs. Sanders, after Mr. Sanders gave up his employment as a horse-keeper in South Kensington because the constant dust from straw in the stables irritated his asthma. Mrs. Clark had many memories of the house at that time. The entrance hall had a fireplace in it opposite the double front doors, and the drawing-room, breakfast room and large conservatory were situated on the right-hand side of it, while the dining-room, billiard-room and small conservatory were on the left. All of the ground-floor front windows had window seats, and shutters to close at night. The second, smaller hallway had panelling on its walls, and the beautiful wrought-iron staircase, with its continuous banister rail from the attic above, provided young Patricia with many good slides down it from top to bottom! There was a door into the panelled gun-room, while in the opposite wall beneath the stairs, another doorway gave access into the cellars, where the secret, underground passage, allegedly to Beddington, was reached through an archway approximately under the large hall, but nobody dared to venture too far along it by candlelight![123]

A rear door in the dining-room led into the servants' passageway, with smaller rooms off it overlooking the courtyard, and the back stairs at the end of it went down into a large kitchen paved with flagstones, and a scullery. This stairway also gave access to first-floor bedrooms and those

42 (*left*): Section of the outer passageway around the large cellar beneath the front right-hand side of Woodcote Hall.
43 (*right*): The small wine cellar under the rear of the front left-hand side of Woodcote Hall.

of the servants, whose quarters were reached through archways at each end of the landing. An indoor toilet and bathroom were by the eastern arch, and there were doorways into storage rooms over the stables at the far ends of both east and west wings.[123]

The inner courtyard had cobble-stones in its centre, and a paved walkway around its perimeter. A large fig-tree grew by the kitchen windows of the east wing. A "privy" stood in the garden outside the entrance archway in the west wing, also there was a vinery here by the walled garden. The well-house and covered well were still *in situ* at the rear of the stables, and the local scouts' meetings were held behind these in grounds owned by St. Patrick's Church, which could be seen from a large window at the end of the eastern wing.[123]

Mrs. Parris was allowed hay from the adjacent meadows, also she kept chickens in the gardens to supply local residents with eggs, and birds for the table which were plucked and prepared in one of the rooms adjoining the archway into the courtyard. Wood and fuel were stored in another room here. After his health had improved, Mr. Sanders travelled around the district each day, and sold fresh fish from a barrow. At the same time, he collected orders for fried fish and chips, which were cooked in the evenings in the brick boiler-house situated beneath ground level near the large conservatory.[123]

Walnut trees grew in a meadow near Woodcote Hall, and the ripe nuts were knocked off the branches so that young Patricia could gather them up. Her schooldays were spent at the new Stanley Park School, then housed in a small building similar to the corrugated-iron church next to it. Each day, she walked there, either along the driveway past the West Lodge occupied by Mr. Hartley, who kept doves, pigeons, and a cow in his garden, and was the coachman at "Woodcote Lodge" in Woodcote Road; or through the woods to the track (Brambledown Road) into the bridle way (Boundary Road) and onwards to Stanley Park Road. At that time a Dr. Scott lived in the East Lodge at the end of the long tree-lined drive to Woodcote Road, and Patricia's step-great-uncle resided in the gardener's cottage (Woodcote Hall Cottage). The Dower House was then used as a school run by a Mr. Doble.[123]

The coronation of George V took place on 22nd June, 1911, and the front of Woodcote Hall was decorated with flags and bunting; also a fair was set up in an adjoining field. Before the celebrations commenced, Mr. and Mrs. Parris had their photograph taken seated in the mansion's entrance porch, with their two daughters, Mrs. Sanders and her sister, on each side of the steps, and Patricia in the background on the right-hand side of the double doors. Probably, this is now the only photographic record of the house before it was altered. Later that day, after Patricia's misbehaviour, she was ordered to remain indoors, but she managed to creep out unobserved to enjoy the fair![123]

The estate agents in charge of Woodcote Hall at that time were Messrs. Finlay Hill, run jointly by three of the Hill brothers, who had their offices in Stanley Park Road on a site next to the one on which the gas showrooms was built some years later. After their eldest brother died in 1911,[123] the two younger partners, Alexander and George Finlay Burd Hill, moved to another office at 18, Woodcote Road.[123, 154] By the end of that year, the Scottish Provident Institution had decided to sell the mansion, and Mr. and Mrs. Parris moved into living-quarters over the coach-house belonging to the Dower House. Mr. Parris obtained employment at the new, large residence in Dower Avenue by Park Hill Road, where he looked after the garden and one cow. Mr. and Mrs. Sanders, with Patricia, had already found another home elsewhere.[123]

Messrs. Finlay Hill became the new owners of Woodcote Hall and just over seven acres of its parklands on 12th February, 1912.[138] Within the next few months they demolished the centre front section of the house containing the double hallways, and the large middle bedroom and attics above them, and formed two residences. The one nearest to Park Hill Road retained the name of "Woodcote Hall", but soon became known as number sixty-six in that road, while the other was re-named "The Old Hall". Most of the wrought-iron spiral staircase was installed in the latter residence, which had the mansion's oldest entrance, on the western side, as its front door. Substantial interior alterations took place in both houses; the exteriors were decorated, and outside shutters added to the ground-floor front windows. The stables were divided equally between the properties, and the well-house was taken down when the well was securely covered over.[96]

There was much speculation among the local residents about the reason for the work on Woodcote Hall. For many years, a rumour had alleged that the ghost of a lady dressed in white occasionally appeared on the main staircase, and, probably, the Scawen/Butterfield affair provided a likely source for this story! Consequently, a new legend arose, and suggested that the middle section of the house had been removed because it was haunted![161] The most logical reason for the drastic alterations was the provision of two smaller residences more attractive to prospective buyers than one large mansion.

Some of the fireplaces were sold during the alterations to Woodcote

44 (*left*): Woodcote Hall. Restoration work on the rear of the middle unit, 1982. 45 (*right*): Woodcote Hall, during restoration of the east wing, 1982.

Hall, and one of these was purchased by a Mr. S. Mayer, who described it as: "a lovely piece of blueish-grey marble and a credit to any house".[162] Unfortunately, the next owners of his residence in Hillside Gardens removed it, probably not appreciating its true value![163]

Messrs. Finlay Hill obtained quick sales for both houses at Woodcote Hall. Joseph R. Carter became the owner of "The Old Hall" on 18th June, 1912, and moved there from "Courtfield" in Ross Road, Wallington. "Woodcote Hall" (66 Park Hill Road) was sold on 19th July, 1912, to Mrs. L.J. Buck, who had just returned to England from Tientsin in North China, with her husband, Mr. R.S. Buck.[138] Plans were drawn up by George F.B. Hill for the seven acres of parkland owned by himself and his brother, and included a new house for them called "Netherfield" in the old walled garden. Part of the sheds here were converted into an extension of the gardener's quarters to form "Woodcote Hall Cottage", and the remainder of them were demolished to provide a garden for this residence;[96] which was let to its first tenant in 1915.[154] Meanwhile, the East Lodge had been pulled down in 1913, and its site used for one of the large properties in Woodcote Road, while the tree-lined driveway became Woodcote Avenue.[164]

In the rural part of Little Woodcote, herbs and lavender grew on the fields in Catsbrain Shott.[156] John Jakson was the tenant of the Little Woodcote Farm until 1914, with just over two hundred and fifty acres of land on which he grew black and white peppermint, chamomile and lavender.[165] Mr. E.C. Pannett, who had bought Stanley House in 1906,[154] established a small herb-drying industry in a building in Fir Tree Grove, at the rear of his residence. He was a partner in Pannett and Needham, the seed merchants, and, because of his trade, his gardens became well-stocked with fruit trees and bushes, as well as many types of flowers. He converted the three attic rooms of his home into a nursery suite with sound-proofed flooring for the younger members of his family. During the First World War, he added an annexe to the house to provide extra accommodation for his daughter and her husband.[166]

After the war, Mr. Pannett sold Stanley House in 1919 to Mr. F. Hosker, who moved there with his wife and two daughters. He had been in service at King Edward VII's court at the beginning of the present century, during which time he travelled to India to act as valet and escort to the sons of a Maharajah on their journey to England, where they received their education. He and his family then moved to South Eaton Place and ran a high-class boarding-house (next to Mr. Enoch Powell's present residence). He acted as the butler, Mrs. Hosker was the cook, and they were assisted by two maids and a footboy. Lord and Lady Hastings, with their three girls, were among their distinguished guests, and regularly attended functions at Buckingham Palace. Another guest, General Boyd, insisted that his money was washed each day before he went out, and so hated the street musicians, so plentiful in those days, that they were forbidden to play outside the house! At the end of their lease in 1914, the Hoskers bought two houses at Wandsworth Common and lived in one, while the other was let to a tenant; until the sale of both properties provided the money to buy Stanley House.[166]

Mr. Hosker and his family were very impressed by the fact that Stanley House seemed quite out of character with its surroundings! A daily woman assisted Mrs. Hosker with the housework, and the ample accommodation here consisted of a large hallway with an oak staircase, on the right-hand side of which was the dining-room covering the full length of the house. At the rear of the hall, double doors with hand-painted glass in them led into the drawing-room overlooking the gardens. On the left of the stairs, the breakfast room had the kitchen behind it, and a hatchway in the ground outside the back door gave access down into a small wine cellar with stone shelves for storage purposes. The large master-bedroom on the first floor was the same size as the dining-room beneath it, and the small room off it was once used as a dressing-room. There were two more bedrooms, a bathroom, and a stairway into the annexe as well as one up to three bedrooms on the second (attic) storey. Until Mr. Hosker's retirement, one of the two gardeners previously employed by Mr. Pannett was retained to tend the large garden, in which grew pear and apple trees, avenues of loganberries and raspberries by a long greenhouse, a mulberry, and one walnut tree. Everyone wore flat shoes on the well-kept lawn with its full-sized tennis court and a section for croquet, and the Hoskers' home became a very popular venue for their relatives and friends.[166]

Meanwhile, Alexander Hill had died at Gallipoli in 1915, during the Dardanelles campaign, and his place in Messrs. Finlay Hill was taken by his brother, John.[167] After the war, he and George F.B. Hill built their new home in Woodcote Avenue as previously planned, but called it "White Craigs" instead of "Netherfield". They bought more of Little Woodcote to sell for further housing developments, and acquired Catsbrain Shott, Windborough Hill Shott and some land in Bramble Shott in 1924.[168]

Mr. Buck's death in March, 1919, caused his widow to sell "Woodcote Hall" (66 Park Hill Road) on 1st September, 1919, to Eric W. Hall,[138] who probably purchased it as an investment, because it remained empty for some while[169] until Mr. Joseph A. Densham became its owner on 9th May, 1921.[138] He employed two gardeners to clear the untended garden, and obtained a strip of land opposite his home along Park Hill Road, from Woodcote Avenue to Brambledown Road, where he grew vegetables until it was divided into plots for houses built during the next fourteen years.[169]

In 1919, Mr. Densham had become a director of the once famous Mazawattee Tea Company, whose offices and adjoining bonded warehouse with the name in gold lettering across its top, stood on Tower Hill, and this and their large factory at New Cross could be seen from trains in and out of London Bridge Station, until they were completely destroyed by bombs in the Second World War (the offices and warehouse in 1940, and the factory in the middle of 1942). The company's origins began locally, in the early 1870s, when, traditionally, Edward and Alfred Densham (trading as Densham & Son) travelled around the Croydon district selling loose tea to various grocers from their box-tricycle. After the introduction of packet tea, they formed the company which, on 4th August, 1896, was handed over to directors who included Mr. Densham's father, John Lane Densham, and uncle, Benjamin Densham. The company's name was the result of Mr. John L. Densham's search at the British Museum, and he put together two words in Tamil – "Maza" meaning luscious, and "Wattee", a garden. He was quite a character, and generous in some ways, but had strict moral principles and belonged to an equally strict Baptist Church. After other firms copied Mazawattee's packet tea, he was involved in the introduction of net-weight laws in this country, because he strongly disagreed with one company's idea of four ounces of tea, which consisted of one and a quarter ounces of lead (the packets were made of lead, which was cheap) and two and three quarter ounces of tea! He allegedly said before the House of Commons Select Committee investigating this case that a false weight was an abomination in the sight of the Lord. He and his wife lived at "Waldronhurst" in Duppas Hill, Croydon (later an hotel), and twelve of their thirteen children survived. As an early enthusiastic motorist, he owned the third car registered in Surrey, BY 3, followed by many others which were housed in his 'motor-house', and lovingly tended by chauffeurs and cleaners employed to look after them.[169]

By the time Joseph Densham became one of the company's directors, his father had died and the new Managing Director was Alexander

Jackson, who introduced some spectacular advertising campaigns. Two vans were drawn by specially imported tame zebras around the City of London, and Dees of Croydon made motorised vans in the shape of a packet of tea, with a tea pot on top and the spout used for the exhaust. He bought a painting, "The Old Folks at Home", depicting an old lady and a little girl enjoying their cups of tea, and registered it as Mazawattee's trade mark. He took out a copyright for their unique "Golden Tips Tea" grown in an Assam garden. The company also specialised in high quality chocolate, cocoa and coffee, had a thriving wholesale chemical concern, and bought-up about twenty other companies to form the Mazawattee Group, including the Decorated Tin Plate Company, who pioneered colour printing on tin. They manufactured tins for the famous pre-war Yardley's Lavender products, and those for the Mazawattee tea and chocolate; and made the Mazawattee advertisements displayed on railway stations, all of which have now become collectors' items. There were Mazawattee factories in South Africa, America and Ireland, and the company was the first to use the Rose's tea packing machines. Mazawattee had a large export trade with Finland, where their "Black Label Golden Tips Tea" was very popular.[169]

In those days, Mazawattee's employees worked long hours. Their offices opened at 8 a.m., and, in sale times or stock-taking, the staff remained there until late evening, and received only one shilling tea money, which was usually spent on beer and sandwiches! The factory workers, including the women, were searched daily before they went home.[169]

At Joseph Densham's home in 66 Park Hill Road, there were what his family called "bullet-proof" shutters inside all of the downstairs windows and, when closed at night, a bar came down to secure them. The beautiful drawing-room and dining-room were connected with a sliding door, and later, when his six children were growing up, tennis parties were held here. There was no central heating, and both rooms were heated by coal fires. The huge kitchens and a wash-house occupied the ground floor of the wing, and, above them, the end room was converted into the children's nursery, where the installation of a large, iron-framed window provided ample light. There were plenty of bedrooms for all of the family, and an additional bathroom was constructed to form a porch over the front door, with its large decorative brass-lion door knocker and surrounding brass wreath. A sun-porch furnished with Lloyd Loom furniture was added on to the side of the residence, and called "The Twiggery". Mr. Densham also built a big double garage in the rear garden to house the family's Rolls Royce, and an Austin Seven for school journeys.[169]

The Denshams' staff consisted of a chauffeur, John Parker, employed to look after and drive the cars; a handyman/gardener, who did not live on the premises; a children's nurse, or nanny; Walter Mason and his wife for the kitchen, and an elderly maid, Lucy. The younger members of the family were forbidden to speak disrespectfully about any of the servants, and Mrs. Densham spent a good deal of her time making and knitting garments for them, as well as collecting items for their Christmas presents. The retired nannies were cared for and visited, or a car sent to fetch them for visits to the house.[169]

Mr. Densham converted his half of the stables into sheds for coal and coke, and the children's budgerigars. There were two large underground rainwater tanks in front of these, and the chauffeur fell into one of them and was nearly drowned when the boards over it gave way! The old fig tree still grew by the kitchen window and chickens were kept in the garden. The family had red setter and Airdale dogs. Maintenance on the house proved to be expensive, especially the large amount of paint required to decorate the exterior (about half a ton in weight) and cost – in those days – £100! The flat parapet on the roof gave continuous trouble, because rainwater collected here and came through on to the bedroom ceilings. The electrical wiring on the old "two pole" system was not earthed, and easily shorted, but less troublesome gas was used for cooking purposes.[169]

The six young Denshams did not have much contact with their parents, but were very fond of their nanny. They spent most of their time with her in the nursery, where they had their meals except for Sunday lunches, and on other important occasions. Sundays were strictly observed with, supposedly, only scriptural books to read, but the three boys found plenty of diversions to keep them occupied in their leisure hours on other days. The path around the house provided a good racing-track for pedal cars and bicycles. At one time, they often climbed out of the toilet window on to the roof's flat parapet to play with their model railway which they had set-up there. It was essential to remember to lock the toilet door on those occasions, otherwise re-entry could prove embarrassing to an unsuspecting occupant, and result in severe reprimands. Expeditions across the low-pitched roof-tops also met with disapproval, because of the danger caused by dislodged slates![169]

The eldest boy, Costin, enjoyed helping John Parker, the chauffeur, with the maintenance work on the cars. In winter, he and his brothers coasted down the hill in Park Hill Road on their toboggan after a fall of snow. As a result of their father's friendship with an ex-naval colleague, who had an electrical business in Wallington, they always had a radio, from the first crystal sets to the more sophisticated types with speakers – and before these came on to the market. Later, their gramophone was converted, so that the sound came out of the radios. One of the earliest telephones in the area was installed in Mr. Densham's home, also he turned part of his front lawn into a tennis court, which became very popular with his children when they grew older.[169]

During the General Strike of 1926 it became very difficult for people to reach their City offices. Mr. Densham transported seven or eight local businessmen up to London in his Rolls Royce. One day, the strikers tried to stop his car in Rye Lane, Peckham, but he bravely confronted them, and greatly impressed his passengers by his adept handling of the situation. They rewarded him with a solid gold match-book in appreciation of his skill in resolving what could have been a very unpleasant incident. At that time, his son, Costin, went to school in a brewery van, which proved more exciting than travelling on a bus![169]

One of Mr. Densham's neighbours, John Hill of Messrs. Finlay Hill, died in Egypt on 25th January, 1925, and left his real and personal estate to his only surviving brother, George,[168] who then moved from "White Craigs" into "Garden Hall Cottage", which he had built on the south-western side of the walled garden. He designed the interior of his home after the style of a medieval hall-house, and to make it look more authentic, he purchased timbers and beams from old cottages which had been demolished on West Country building sites. A coat of arms removed from Woodcote Hall in 1912 was placed in a rockery in his garden (and can be seen here today); and a barn with a pantiled roof was converted into a garage for his car.[96] He had another residence in the Great Park of Peel, near Busby in Lanarkshire, Scotland, and divided his time between there and his house in Wallington.[96, 167]

Mr. Carter died on 22nd May, 1926, and left "The Old Hall" to his wife, Eliza, who only survived him for about eight months before her own death occurred on 13th January, 1927. She left the house to her son and daughter, W.J. Brabrook Carter and Beatrice, who sold it to Mr. Harry D. Burton on the following 18th May.[138] He and his wife set up a private preparatory school for boys here, and caused Mr. Densham to replace his laurel hedge between the two gardens with a high wooden fence, because the schoolboys refused to return any tennis balls which fell over there.[169]

Costin Densham and his friend Peter became interested in the legend of Woodcote Hall's secret passageway to Carshalton Park, and decided to try and trace it. They searched for its entrance in the small cellar beneath Costin's home, but found only a bricked-up archway. They explored the school's large, dark cellars, without success, while the Burtons were away on their holidays, but quickly left there because of the sinister atmosphere![169]

Quite a number of aeroplanes crashed in the district during the years following the commencement of early commercial air traffic at Croydon Airport in 1920. One such incident occurred on ground at the rear of St. Patrick's Church while Costin and his eldest sister, Mary, were playing tennis. They rushed to the scene of the accident, but were severely shocked to find that the 'plane's occupants were dead, and suffered for some weeks from the after-effects of that horrible scene. The famous "Captain Kettle" of Imperial Airways, Captain O.P. Jones, investigated the crash, and when he called to interview them was invited to stay for tea.[169]

In 1933, Costin joined the Mazawattee Tea Company and remained with them until he entered the armed services in the Second World War. His father became the company's Managing Director after Mr. Jackson's death in 1934, but the Wall Street Crash adversely affected his own finances and those of the company. Mr. Burton's school at "The Old Hall" had never been a profitable business, and the depression of the early thirties influenced his decision to sell the house to local building contractors,[169] Messrs. Hollands & Boakes, and the sale was completed on 9th February, 1935.[138]

By 1935, Mr. Densham's life-style at 66 Park Hill Road was difficult to maintain. He had never really liked the ostentation of the house, and had few regrets when he decided to sell it[169] to Messrs. Hollands & Boakes on 30th April, 1935,[138] and moved into a smaller property in Woodcote Avenue called "Stradella". His company's finances improved with the introduction of tea rationing in the war, and on the loss of their offices, bonded warehouse, and factory, they used office space provided by Furness Withy, a shipping company in Fenchurch Street, while Brooke Bond packed their tea for them for the period of hostilities. In post-war years, Mr. Densham was forced by illness to retire, but he had already received a presentation clock for his fifty years' service. He was replaced by a man from outside the company, due to the ageing board of directors, and lack of suitable younger, experienced people within the business, after two wars had removed potential candidates.[169]

The new Managing Director's different ideas and principles led to his disposal of Mazawattee's New Cross factory site, and, after he obtained a majority of voting shares, he completed a quick "take-over" deal with a biscuit company, and left the country with a large tax-free sum of money! Tragically, the other directors lost their jobs, security and pensions, and Mr. Densham was deprived of nearly all of his financial investments in the firm. The new owners gradually allowed the once-famous name of Mazawattee to lapse.[169] Meanwhile, Woodcote Hall had entered another phase in its history, and more changes took place on its former estate.

CHAPTER 11

NEW BEGINNINGS

In contrast to the suburban developments in northern Little Woodcote between the wars, the southern end of the estate retained its rural scenery. The Surrey County Council had launched a scheme of smallholdings here for some of the ex-servicemen who found difficulties in obtaining employment on leaving the armed services. The County Council already owned part of the Old Lodge in Greater Woodcote, and had erected a few houses near Woodcote Green in 1912.[156] From August 1919, they purchased Windborough Hill Shott, Milton Hill, Tanner's Piece, Scotch Piece, and Heycott Bottom, as well as Maiden's Grave, to form their new "Little Woodcote Estate".[70] The two dwellings in the old farmhouse became Little Woodcote Cottages, and the later farmhouse became known as "The Old Lodge Farm"; and the tenements here gradually disappeared over the next thirty years, except for a single-storey building in the farmyard.[126]

The new owners of Woodcote Hall, Charles Boakes and his brother-in-law, Spencer Hollands, had arrived in Wallington in the early 1920s and established themselves here as Messrs. Hollands & Boakes.[170] When they bought 66 Park Hill Road and "The Old Hall", they were already involved in some of the re-developments on the former northern part of Little Woodcote. Their new block of shops and flats designed by Mr. Hollands had been completed on the site of "Shotfield" on the corner of Beddington Gardens (south side) and Woodcote Road, and they had their new offices at 9 Beddington Gardens.[96] In early April, 1933, Sir John Bletso performed the opening ceremony of their new South London Motors' showrooms, with self-contained flats on the two floors above it, which they had built after the demolition of "Cottesbrook" in Stafford Road by Woodcote Road. The *Wallington Herald* of 7th April, 1933, described the building as one of the largest of its kind in Surrey, and the occasion was featured in the *Wallington Times, Croydon Advertiser* and *The Motor* of the same date. They had commenced work on the adjacent Public Hall complex, where the late

Sir Edward Braybrook's home, "Langham House", had been demolished.[171] Mr. Boakes's son Leslie was in charge of the building operations, and, on completion, he ran the Hall until after the Second World War, when it was taken over by Beddington and Wallington Council.[96]

Other re-developments took place in Woodcote Road. The large residences opposite the shops and "Rosemount" were demolished to provide sites for the gas showrooms, more shopping facilities, and a Town Hall, which was opened in September, 1935. The opening ceremony of a new, single-storey library at the rear of it was held on 3rd October, 1936.[171] These two public buildings stood on the site of "Sunnybank", which had been used as Council Offices since 1929.[159]

In the early 1930s, Mr. Hosker, at Stanley House, sold part of his large garden for the first St. Margaret's Church, which stood on ground previously used for the avenue of loganberries and the long greenhouse.[166] In 1932, more of his property, by Fir Tree Grove, was bought by Mr. J. Vinn, who erected four bungalows on it after legal problems about a right-of-way had been resolved.[166, 172] Mr. Hosker's shrubbery provided a site for the shops in Stanley Road, as well as a garage for his nephews, who lived in the adjoining residence.[166]

Messrs. Hollands & Boakes carried out a good deal of work at 66 Park Hill Road and "The Old Hall" during 1935-36. They converted both properties into self-contained flats, and built one unit in the space between the fronts of them to give an outward appearance of a single house again, which was re-named Woodcote Hall. They divided the larger rooms into smaller ones, removed the wrought-iron staircase, added a bathroom on to the east wing (which became a three-bedroomed residence), and turned the western one into two units, where they installed panelling from Shoolbreds of London, and incorporated the archway into the new ground-floor accommodation. Demolition of the stable block provided a site for a rose garden, and the two pillars from the old entrance portico pulled down in 1912 were cut in half and used to decorate the front unit's façade, where an arched passage provided access into the courtyard. Mr. Boakes's son Leslie became involved with the conversion work, and, from then onwards, took a particular interest in the old mansion.[96]

By the beginning of 1936, tenants had moved into the first two completed units on the front, eastern side of Woodcote Hall, and they were able to watch the building operations in progress.[173] An old hitching-post for horses stood just inside the archway into the courtyard, which was paved with small oblong cobbles set on edge.[161] The entrance to an underground passage at the rear of the stables was visible, as well as one to a passageway beneath the front of the house. The former supposedly led to the caves at Beddington, and the latter to Carshalton. Both of the entrances were bricked-up, also some foundations of an older house were uncovered at that time.[173]

Other units at Woodcote Hall were quickly occupied on completion.[173] In the following years, the tenants became a very happy, small community.[174] A group of them have remained in contact with each other after their respective departures, and have enjoyed their annual reunions since then. Some of them were interested in the history of the house during their periods of residence there, and joined the local archaeological society. One lady, who was intrigued by the legend of the underground passage to Carshalton House, called at St. Philomena's School, where she was shown what was, allegedly, the other end of it![175] A few local tradesmen were able to provide some interesting details, and the laundryman, who was eighty years old, remembered a herd of deer in the parklands when he was a young boy. The elderly coalman's uncle (who was even older), had been the bailiff of Little Woodcote, and lived in a cottage at the south-western corner of the walled garden (later Woodcote Hall Cottage).[176]

Woodcote Hall's legendary "White Lady" had little effect upon the tenants, some of whom remained unaware of her ghostly presence! However, after the removal of a cupboard in a ground-floor front room, strange knocking noises began, but ceased when these were attributed to her![173] The occupants of another unit enjoyed playing chess, and alleged that if an unfinished game was left overnight, the chessmen had been moved several times by morning, or the chessboard was found on the floor with the pieces undisturbed![170] Perhaps the "Lady" was a proficient chess-player in her earthly life?

In pre-war years, there were few disadvantages for Woodcote Hall's tenants, except those with the large, high, front rooms, which were difficult to heat in winter, but a plentiful supply of logs could be obtained from the woods nearby before the trees were cut down to make way for more property developments.[173] During the war, Leslie Boakes became a Civil Defence Instructor and was in charge of a Heavy Rescue Squad. He took his men to London in the "blitz" and assisted with the recovery of people trapped beneath the debris of bombed buildings. He also included the care of Woodcote Hall's occupants in his duties, and although bombs fell in the vicinity of the house, only minor damage was sustained,[170] even when a flying-bomb (the V1 known colloquially as a "Doodle-bug") fell in Hall Road and damaged many properties in the area.

Woodcote Hall, West Lodge, Garden Hall and Woodcote Hall Cottages, the Old Lodge Farm, and Little Woodcote Cottages, all survived the war years, although the latter had an aircraft factory near them on the edge of the woods in Woodmansterne Lane, and propellers were manufactured there. It became a target for enemy bombers, so that many bombs were dropped on the smallholdings! Italian prisoners-of-war arrived daily on the Little Woodcote Estate to assist with the agricultural work in place of young men in the armed services. Before the hostilities ceased, the Italians moved elsewhere and were replaced by Germans.

At Stanley House, Mr. Hosker converted his small wine cellar beneath the kitchen into an air-raid shelter. Mrs. Hosker died after the war, and he let some of the rooms in his home to tenants, but lived here until his death.[166] His son sold the house in 1959 to Messrs. Farren Estates, who then converted it into flats.[177] Its surroundings were improved after Carshalton Council demolished "Jerusalem" and built smaller dwellings on its site. Gale and Alexandra Terraces, and Phoenix House, were pulled down and replaced by Alexandra Gardens, and a block of private flats stood on ground previously occupied by Stanley Villas.

In post-war years, Little Woodcote Cottages came under private ownership again, when purchased from Surrey County Council by the present owner's father in 1951. Tenants occupied one of the dwellings at that time, but were soon re-housed, and the owner's son moved there from the Old Lodge Farm, where he had been a tenant since 1934 after it had been re-built following a fire which destroyed the late nineteenth-century house.[126]

After restrictions on building materials were removed, property developments began again on available empty land around Woodcote Hall. The old corrugated-iron St. Patrick's Church had already been replaced by a new brick-built one in 1933, and work commenced on a church hall in 1966, which covered the site of the large draw-well. Re-developments have taken place on the former northern section of Little Woodcote. Blocks of flats have replaced many of the large houses in Woodcote Road and those in other adjacent roads. Local residents have sold parts of their gardens for more housing, and a tower block and shopping precinct took over the site of "Rosemount" in Wallington.

Charles Boakes died in 1964, and Spencer Hollands in early 1966. Messrs. Hollands & Boakes passed to Leslie and his cousin, Ray Hollands, but because the firm was not involved in any more large building projects, Mr. Boakes became the active member of the partnership, while Mr. Hollands continued with his career as an architect. Leslie's wife died in July, 1966, after a marriage of over thirty years, during which time they had two daughters. He remained a widower until December, 1969, when he married his second wife, Hylda.[170]

In 1972, the death occurred of another gentleman who had played a significant part in the history of Woodcote Hall and the development of its estate. Mr. George F.B. Hill, known to his many friends as "Finlay Hill", died on 5th July in that year at his residence in the Great Park of Peel, near Busby, Lanarkshire, at the age of ninety-two. He was born in March 1880, and had seen many changes take place in Wallington during his lifetime. In the early part of his career he became an Associate Member of the Royal Institution of Chartered Surveyors in 1907, and a Member in 1909. As a modest man of immense character and integrity, he gained the respect of all who knew him, and his concern for improving the standard of living for under-privileged young people led to his involvements with the Scout movement in East London, and the Boys' Brigade in Glasgow.[167] He retired to his Scottish property in later life, but retained the ownership of both Garden Hall Cottage and Woodcote Hall Cottage until his death,[96] when the trustee of his will sold these properties.[167]

In February 1974, Messrs. Hollands & Boakes were notified by the Department of the Environment of Woodcote Hall's inclusion in the statutory list of buildings of special architectural, or historical, interest, compiled by the Secretary of State. By October 1974, the London Borough of Sutton's Secretary's Department had informed them that the house was a Grade II listed building under Section 54 of the Town & Country Planning Act of 1971, which meant that it was considered important enough to warrant every effort made to preserve its outer appearance.[96] All of the first group of tenants had moved elsewhere, but those who replaced them had always maintained the former, happy, community spirit.[170]

Due to escalating costs for the maintenance and upkeep of Woodcote Hall, and with only a limited income from its tenants to support it, the condition of the house deteriorated during the last years of Leslie Boakes's life, and caused him much concern. Before he could carry out the plans he had made to obtain some money towards the restoration work required on the building,[96] he died on 19th July, 1979, and his two daughters inherited his share of the partnership of Messrs. Hollands & Boakes. Woodcote Hall's affairs were put in the hands of local estate agents, Messrs. Reed & Woods, and they were given instructions to sell it.[170]

Leslie Boakes had led an active and interesting life. He was born and educated in West Ham, and had just left school when he arrived in Wallington. His first employment was at the Smithfield Meat Market, and during the General Strike of 1926 he walked to work and always arrived on time; and at the end of the day he then set out on foot to return home! Next, he became an office boy with Messrs. Dewhursts, and after joining his father in Hollands & Boakes, he studied for and obtained his Fellowship of the Institute of Builders. After the war, he was a member of the local Rotary Club and a Rotarian for over thirty years, as well as a Past President of Wallington's Rotarians.[170]

Many people will remember Leslie for his long association with, and work for, the local Scouts' groups. He was awarded the Silver Acorn in 1975 for his fifty years' service in the Scout movement, and attended the National Scouts' St. George's Day Service in St. George's Chapel at Windsor Castle, on Sunday, 20th April, 1975, an honour reserved for those who have received this award. By then, he was Chairman of the Carshalton and Wallington District Scouts. He also found time to assist with the administration of the Wallington Division of Girl Guides as their treasurer from 1963 onwards. In 1978, he was given the Greater London West County Award for his hard work on behalf of the Guide movement, and was the first man to receive this honour. Unfortunately, he had become ill by then, and, reluctantly, gave up all of the activities he had carried out with so much enthusiasm. He was seventy years of age when he died, and was greatly missed by all of his friends.[170]

Woodcote Hall remained on the market for nearly two years, until one day in June, 1981, David Jackson, of Messrs. Granville Builders Limited, paid a casual visit to the estate agents, Reed & Woods. During his conversation with Brian Reed, Mr. Jackson remarked that he wished to do something different in his work which would present him with a challenge, and Mr. Reed persuaded him to buy the house and restore it! Afterwards, he became interested in its historical background, and, on seeing some old plans of it, conceived the idea of building four houses on the site of the stable block, so that, once again, the inner courtyard would be enclosed.[178]

The sale of Woodcote Hall was completed on 12th August, 1981, and David Jackson began his tremendous task of restoring its exterior and modernising its interior; but he had found the challenge he so eagerly sought! However, the work did not proceed without some problems, including the cold winter of 1981/82. In the summer of 1982, while preparing the ground for the foundations of the four new houses on the site of the old stabling, the driver of the mechanical digger was dismayed to find that both he and the machine were slowly sinking into the earth. After completion of successful rescue operations, the incident led to the discovery of the large double water container beneath the footings of the stables. Next, the same enthusiastic workman, although slightly shaken by his unusual experience, uncovered and damaged a big cable here, thus gaining the displeasure of his employer, and the Electricity Board![178]

David Jackson had sole charge of Woodcote Hall just before completion of all work on the site in 1983. Apart from his working life, he is very much a family man. Both he and his wife, Barbara, were born in Sutton, but have lived in Wallington for some years. Their eldest daughter, Susan, is married, and their son, Stephen, lives with them and their youngest girl, Samantha, who is described as the "apple of her father's eye"! Mrs. Jackson is interested in local history, and her own family, the Snellings, had a furniture business in Sutton from 1890 until recently, when their premises in West Street were demolished together with others in that road, to provide a site for a car park. David's main hobby is scuba diving, for which he has his own sea-worthy boat. He has commenced looking for treasure under the sea, after an unsuccessful search for Woodcote Hall's secret underground passage which, allegedly, once had some diamonds hidden in its door![178] Most of the units and houses here have been sold, and, perhaps, the new owner/occupiers will have their own story to relate in a future chapter of the history of the house.

IN SEARCH OF HISTORY

From early 1980 until 1983, a number of investigatory visits to Woodcote Hall were made by arrangement with Mr. Brian Reed of Messrs. Reed & Woods, and the kind permission of Mr. Ray Hollands, and with that of Mr. David Jackson during the restoration and modernisation work. The opportunities to explore the house and collect invaluable information, the help and interest of the tenants, the site foreman and his men, were greatly appreciated.

Preparations for the modernisation work on the interior of Woodcote Hall exposed traces of previous, smaller houses on the site, and the oldest parts were discovered in and near the east wing. Before the exterior restoration began, the different sections of brickwork seen on the outer, western wall suggested that, at one time, access into the courtyard was gained through a gap between the front part of the building and the west wing. The location of the earlier main entrance to the house was identified from marks left by the removal of the doorcase, and a well-worn step beneath them (see diagram 1). The door was replaced by a window in 1935, when some of the old crown glass from a decorative fanlight was placed above it.[96] Small yellow bricks set on edge were found beneath the soil and indicated the position of the archway through the west wing, while faint outlines of beams around it showed its height and width. The roofs of both wings were covered with Horsham tiles.

Daniel Burrell's map of 1818 shows some recesses in the walls at the front of the house and rear of the stables (see diagram 2). Because these conflict with Robert Mylne's alterations here in the late eighteenth century, they could indicate the old building line, or foundations left beneath floor levels at that time.

The large cellar under the front right-hand side of Woodcote Hall was cool, and well-ventilated by two gratings placed at ground level in the northern, outer wall. The whole area measured forty-six feet in length and thirty-seven feet five inches in width, divided into two equal sections, but the one nearest the middle of the house had another two

WOODCOTE LODGE

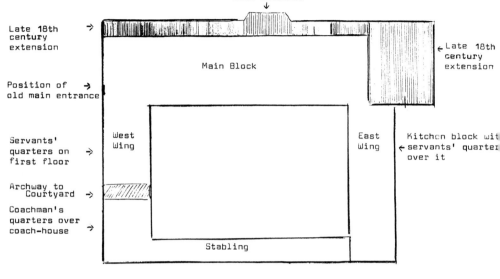

Late 18th century
main entrance
↓

Late 18th
century
extension →

←Late 18th
century
extension

Main Block

Position of →
old main entrance

West
Wing

East
Wing

Kitchen block wit
←servants' quarter
over it

Servants'
quarters on →
first floor

Archway to
    Courtyard →

Coachman's
quarters over →
coach-house

Stabling

✗ Draw-well

ENLARGED PLAN OF WOODCOTE LODGE TAKEN
TAKEN FROM DANIEL BURRELL'S SURVEY MAP OF 1818

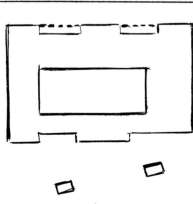

sub-divisions in it (see diagram 3). The floor was paved with bricks, except for the small, north-eastern section, where it consisted of hard rubble, and the inner dividing wall had a rough surface on its northern face, which suggested that it was part of the base of an older, smaller building as well as conforming to one of the recesses shown on Daniel Burrell's map (see diagrams 2 and 3). Some of the old timbered framework of the seventeenth century west wing was exposed in the left-hand wall by the top of the entrance stairway, and the carpenter's marks on the wood were visible (see diagram 3).

One of Woodcote Hall's most unusual features is its arched, underground passage around the exterior walls of the large cellar. It is made of bricks, and projects outwards from the main outside wall, onto which its roof joins at a point just below ground level. It has a curved outer wall and a channel along its base (see diagram 4). Five archways provide access into it; two on the western side, one behind the stairway and another two in the inner rear wall, where it had been broken down when the building line was extended into the courtyard in 1912 (see diagram 3). It does not continue around the perimeter of the older west wing, but is blocked up by a brick wall where this section joins the front of the house, and a gully here is sited beneath the cellar's floor level.

The passageway must be attributed to part of Robert Mylne's work on the house. It was constructed as an ingenious form of damp-course to protect the base of the outside walls, which, otherwise, would be subjected to excessive dampness, because the building is situated on the slopes of the hillside. (This type of damp-course is still used today in similar circumstances.[179]) During visits to the large cellar on rainy days, rainwater ran down the arched outside walls of the outer passage into the curved base, along which it was carried away without touching the brickwork of the main walls below ground. There is a drainage point in its front section, with a small gully that disappears under the cellar floor towards the courtyard, where the remains of another passage leading to the stable block were also uncovered during the restoration work.

An exterior gully replaced the demolished portion of the passageway at the rear of the cellar, and runs beneath the ground outside the later building line, down into the small section of the passage behind the entrance stairway, where there is a deeper channel for collection of water than found elsewhere, although it does not appear to have an outlet. However, a cylindrical brick container, or "well", was discovered on this side of the courtyard and, from the position of an opening in its northern wall, it seemed the likely receptacle for rainwater from the

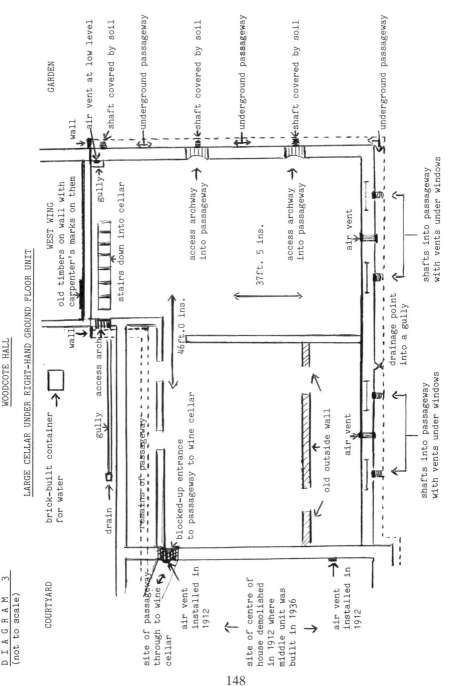

DIAGRAM 3
(not to scale)

WOODCOTE HALL

LARGE CELLAR UNDER RIGHT-HAND GROUND FLOOR UNIT

brick-built container
for water

GARDEN

wall
air vent at low level
shaft covered by soil
underground passageway
shaft covered by soil
underground passageway
shaft covered by soil
underground passageway

WEST WING
old timbers on wall with
carpenter's marks on them
gully
stairs down into cellar

access archway
into passageway

37ft. 5 ins.

access archway
into passageway

air vent

shafts into passageway
with vents under windows

FRONT OF HOUSE

COURTYARD

gully
access arch
drain
remains of passageway
blocked-up entrance
to passageway to wine cellar

wall

46ft.0 ins.

old outside wall

air vent

drainage point
into a gully

shafts into passageway
with vents under windows

site of passageway
through to wine
cellar
air vent
installed in
1912

site of centre of
house demolished
in 1912 where
middle unit was
built in 1936

air vent
installed in
1912

148

E — W

deepest section of the damp-course (see diagram 3).

Adequate ventilation of the passageway is provided by four air shafts in the northern section of its roof (three in the western part were covered with soil) and the gratings for these were found in the paving beneath each of the front windows. Corresponding vents are situated in the outer wall of the house below ground level and provide good air circulation in both passage and the cellar (see diagram 4).

There is no large cellar under the front left-hand side of Woodcote Hall, and no traces of an indented wall as shown on Daniel Burrell's map. Part of the building is supported on two lines of brickwork running from east to west, in which arches are placed at regular intervals, but, beneath the eastern end, support is given by brick walls built in the same direction, as well as three more from north to south. All of these have small square holes in them for ventilation provided by two gratings at ground level in the outer wall. A shallow damp-course passage runs along the frontage here, and another one underneath it is at the same level as the passageway around the large cellar, with similar ventilation shafts under each window.

The small wine cellar beneath this side of Woodcote Hall is situated under the oldest part of it near the courtyard and east wing. The curved wooden staircase down into its entrance passageway has not been used since the house was divided into flats in 1935. Some of its floor is made up of brick paving and the remainder is paved with stone flags, part of which were once covered with a dark glazing. It has four sections of unequal proportions on each side, and the remains of old iron supports for shelving can be seen in the walls. The whole area is covered by a vaulted roof (see diagram 5).

The length of the cellar is thirteen feet four inches, including an end alcove, which is forty-two inches wide, and seventeen inches deep. Its overall width is twelve feet six inches, and it is ten feet five inches in height at the centre of its vaulted roof. A brick and slate gully, six and a half inches high, and six inches wide, runs beneath the floor at an angle from north-east to south-west, and curves away towards the courtyard by the steps at the western end. The entrance passage from the stairs is also angled in roughly the same direction (see diagram 5 for measurements).

The wine cellar extends only as far as an interior wall which was once the outer eastern one of a smaller, older house on the site. There is a grating at high level in an alcove here, through which a bricked-up arched entrance can be seen, suggesting that, at one time, access could

D I A G R A M   4.
(not to scale)

VERTICAL SECTION OF FRONT OF LARGE CELLAR.

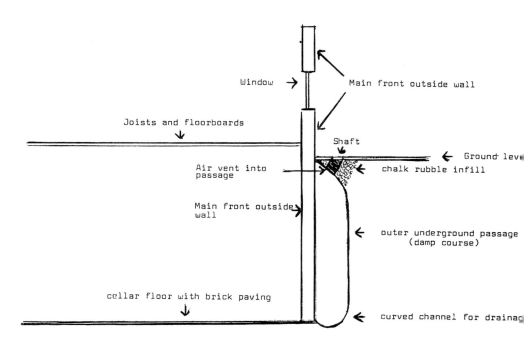

Window →

Main front outside wall

Joists and floorboards

Shaft

Ground level

Air vent into
passage

chalk rubble infill

Main front outside
wall

outer underground passage
(damp course)

cellar floor with brick paving

curved channel for drainage

be gained either from outside the mansion, or from the kitchen quarters in the east wing. Another blocked-up archway by the stairs led into a passage beneath the centre of the house which was used before 1912 to reach the large cellar (see diagram 5).

During the modernisation of the ground floor unit immediately above the wine cellar, some interesting features were exposed when the wall nearest to the middle of the house was stripped down to the brickwork. In the north-west (front) corner, the surface of the bricks was smooth and had been painted, although the original colour was hard to define because it had become a dark yellowish-brown with age and dust, but the pointing had been carefully and evenly completed. Therefore, this could be part of an exterior wall to an older house and, again, would conform to the plan on Daniel Burrell's map. Towards the interior of the room, it was possible to see the position of the arch over the entrance to the dining room from the hallway of the eighteenth-century house, also there were two infills of breeze blocks on each side of the fireplace where windows had been sited after 1912. The whole area was covered with vertical lines of battens, and remains of a second, more modern line of bricks in the south-west corner suggested that the wall had been strengthened for use as an outer one (see diagram 6). Immediately above this section, it was possible to see up to the roof, and traces of different, lower ceiling levels and an arched doorway were visible, as well as evidence of a second storey above the first floor.

At the same time, it was possible to examine the former exterior eastern wall of an older house here, because part of it had been exposed in the same ground-floor unit on this side of Woodcote Hall. This wall had been constructed in two sections and was approximately eighteen inches in thickness. The end wall of the wine cellar could be seen here, with the bricked-up arched entrance and grating above it. The thickest walls, which measured just over two feet in parts of them, were found on the Park Hill Road side of the east wing, which dates from the sixteenth century. Despite the alterations made to its rooms since 1912, these still have low doorways and ceiling levels, which are also features of the west wing.

There are two lofts over the left-hand front section of Woodcote Hall. In the oldest one nearest to the middle of the house, the timbers show four alterations to the roof here. At first, there was a high-pitched open one, without any attics; secondly, the top of it was cut off and a slightly barrel-shaped centre added to it; thirdly, the joists with vertical holds showed the remains of a ceiling on them where attics had been installed.

151

SMALL WINE CELLAR AT WOODCOTE HALL

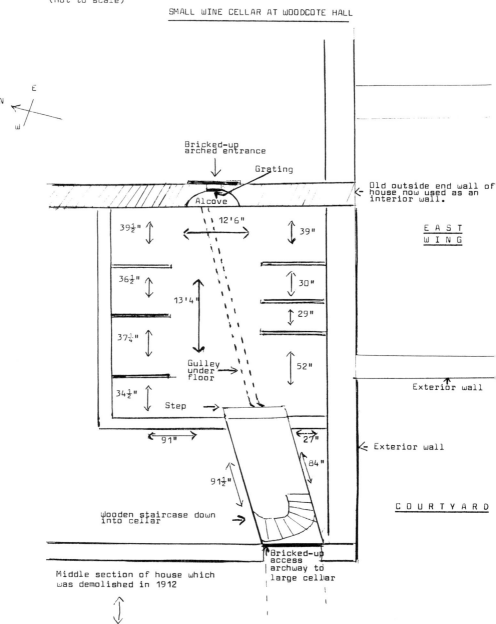

Bricked-up
arched entrance

Grating

Alcove

Old outside end wall of
house now used as an
interior wall.

E A S T
W I N G

39½"

12'6"

39"

36½"

13'4"

30"

29"

37¼"

Gulley
under
floor

52"

34½"

Step

91"

27"

Exterior wall

84"

Exterior wall

91½"

C O U R T Y A R D

Wooden staircase down
into cellar

Bricked-up
access
archway to
large cellar

Middle section of house which
was demolished in 1912

The fourth and present low-pitched stage was made when the front of the building was extended outwards, and a different means of support was then required for the rafters above it. Hand-made nails and very large nuts and bolts were used to prevent the roof from spreading, and fastened the rafters on to a huge piece of wood, which rested only on the tops of the interior walls, with the vertical tie stronger than the horizontal one, and other pieces of timber were wedged between them to allow for ventilation.[180]

In the second loft over the front eastern end of Woodcote Hall, the timbers were constructed for the fourth, low-pitched stage of the roof only, which was part of Robert Mylne's design for the house. A blocked-up window was discovered in the former exterior wall, and once provided light for the end attic room in the first loft.[180] Recently, it was possible to examine the roof construction in the two sections of the loft over the right-hand front part of the house. In the one nearest to the middle unit, similar features to those in the oldest loft on the opposite side were found, as well as a disused chimney-breast (with no hearths below) from an older building on the site. The second section has a mix of timbers, some of which have been re-used for the low-pitched stage, forming a collar to triangulate the rafters for stability. The roof here has a noticeable double pitch; and the north-west shallow half-hip is repeated at the south-western end. Part of the exposed brickwork consists of English bond on top of Flemish bond, with more modern bricks used for the front addition. The position of an old fire-place in the west wall is visible behind the modern one.[188]

There is a large cylindrical brick container under the lawn at the north-eastern front corner of Woodcote Hall. Its small opening at the top is covered by a grating, and, with allowance for any sediment in the bottom of it, its depth is approximately twelve feet. The water in it is just below ground level, and is a considerable height above the old water table, which suggests that it is a receptacle for rainwater from the damp-course system around and beneath the house and courtyard.

Some of the disused older types of drains were found beneath the floors of both cellars at Woodcote Hall. A few of these were exposed in an excavation in the courtyard near the east wing during the modernisation work, and some of the foundations of an older house were uncovered in the same hole.

When the large underground rainwater container by the footings of the old stables had been emptied, it was possible to see that it had been constructed with red bricks, some of which were the older, soft type. It was eleven feet square and approximately six feet deep, and a large sheet of iron placed from north to south divided it into two equal sections. It appeared to be another receptacle for the water collected in the underground damp-course system. The footings behind it at the eastern end of the trenches were about two feet in thickness, which indicated that these were another part of the oldest building on the site.

More old foundations were uncovered at the southern end of the east and west wings, as well as the remains of an underground passage along the rear of the stables (this allegedly went to the caves in Beddington). Pieces of pottery, china, glassware, bottles and bones were discovered beneath the roots of an evergreen tree, which was removed on the western side of the site. From the approximate age of the tree, these finds were dated to about the first half of the nineteenth century.

Another interesting feature was exposed in the trenches dug out for the foundations of the garages at the side of Woodcote Hall. The concave outline of a ditch could be seen in the chalk strata, and this had been filled in with soil many years ago to level the ground. Possibly it was the course of an old stream which once flowed down the hill in approximately the same position (as shown on a map in *The Story of Wallington and its Parish Church*, page 17, by H.V. Molesworth Roberts [British Publishing Co. Ltd., 1937]). After the stream dried up, the ditch was probably used for drainage purposes, or to prevent any cattle from straying out of the parklands into the gardens around the house. Lastly, a section of old bricks laid on edge was discovered under the disused rockery in the garden by the corner of Woodcote Avenue and Park Hill Road, and it appeared to be part of the old forecourt.

By kind permission of the owners, visits were made to other existing houses which were part of old Little Woodcote. The single-storey section of Woodcote Hall Cottage presents some very interesting features. The eastern side is made up of part of the old wall surrounding the walled garden, and, therefore, contains several types of bricks of various dates from the sixteenth century onwards. One of the supporting buttresses is visible, and the modern brickwork can be seen just below the roof. The windows on the western side have been adapted from those which let light into the sheds, and include one placed in a bricked-up doorway. The front wall and door face north, and were built by Messrs. Finlay Hill after 1912, when other buildings here were demolished to provide a garden for the cottage.[49]

The largest part of the house is at the rear, and has accommodation on two floors. Its southern wall curves round to conform with the old

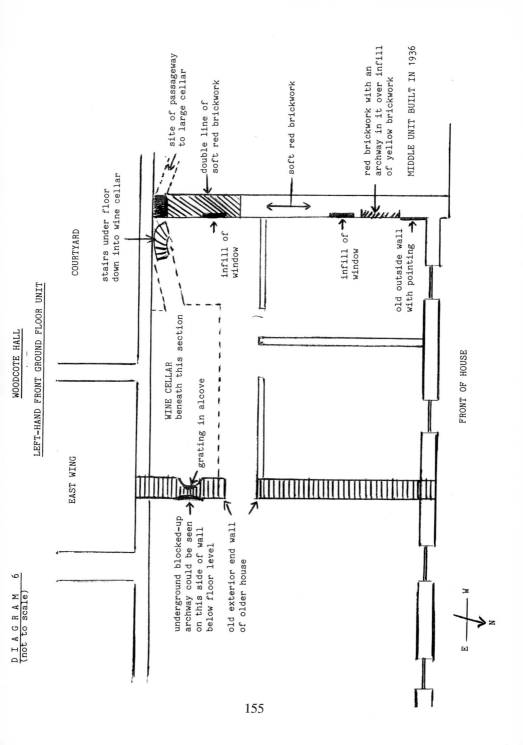

DIAGRAM 6
(not to scale)

WOODCOTE HALL

LEFT-HAND FRONT GROUND FLOOR UNIT

EAST WING

COURTYARD

stairs under floor
down into wine cellar

site of passageway
to large cellar

double line of
soft red brickwork

infill of
window

WINE CELLAR
beneath this section

grating in alcove

underground blocked-up
archway could be seen
on this side of wall
below floor level

old exterior end wall
of older house

soft red brickwork

infill of
window

red brickwork with an
archway in it over infill
of yellow brickwork

MIDDLE UNIT BUILT IN 1936

old outside wall
with pointing

FRONT OF HOUSE

N

E — W

155

building-line of the walled garden; consequently, the roof over it has wide, projecting eaves. The brickwork has been covered over and painted: therefore it was not possible to see traces of the alterations carried out on it since the late eighteenth century. Inside the cottage, there are different floor levels in part of the ground-floor, which indicate various sections of the old sheds where farm horses, implements, carts and wagons were kept.[49]

West Lodge in Woodcote Avenue marks the site of the western entrance to the driveway to Woodcote Hall from the old Bridle Way (now Boundary Road) but its use as a gatehouse ceased just over one hundred years ago.[148, 152, 153] Since the early part of the present century, various owners have enlarged the house and carefully preserved its oldest sections. In the 1920s, extra accommodation was added on to its western side, and other additions at the rear of it have taken place in the last sixteen years. The three rooms in the octagonal section were converted into one large sitting-room, with a central fireplace and chimney, and the late eighteenth-century rafters in the roof here have been kept in good condition.[65]

The oldest part of West Lodge, which dates from the seventeenth century, is situated at the rear of the octagonal section, and once contained two rooms for the gatekeeper and his family. Its special features are a large old door, the original fireplace with its exterior crooked chimney, and the small windows in the eastern wall (see diagram 7).[65]

When the octagonal part of West Lodge was added in the late eighteenth century, there were round bulls-eye windows in six of the eight sections, but shortly afterwards one of these was blocked up, probably to avoid the window tax introduced at that time.[96] The original design of them was lost during the last sixteen years, when they were renewed because the wooden frames had deteriorated with age. At the same time, the front door was moved to the eastern side of the house, but the replacement window and wall were carefully matched to conform with the other sections of the octagon. The bay-window in the western addition was replaced by a pseudo-Georgian one, and there were more alterations and additions to the rear rooms.[65]

Towards the end of the Second World War, West Lodge became the home of a local artist, Miss Sheila Ellis, who taught needlework at the former Wallington County School for Girls in Stanley Park Road.[181] Her paintings of this small house have captured forever its original gothic doorway, the old bulls-eye windows, the crooked chimney on the oldest

WEST LODGE

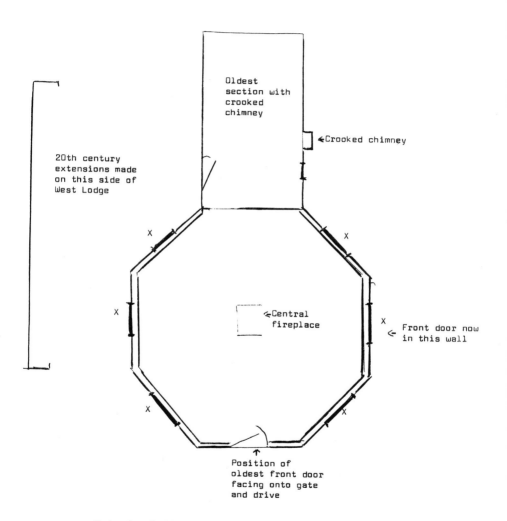

Oldest section with crooked chimney

←Crooked chimney

20th century extensions made on this side of West Lodge

←Central fireplace

X

X

X

X

X

X

←Front door now in this wall

↑
Position of oldest front door facing onto gate and drive

X denotes "bull's-eye" windows

part of the building, and her delightful "cottage garden".[182]

One half of the Little Woodcote farmhouse has been modernised in recent years, because the front wall became unsafe and had to be rebuilt.[183] The exterior of the other part of the house has been left unchanged; and the windows with some of the old crown glass in them, as well as the arched front doorway, are typical of Mylne's gothic designs.[114] The interior walls are made up of wood and bricks[126] and all of the rooms have low ceiling levels and wide doorways. The front door has a large chain attached to its inner side, and another old door has been preserved. Also, there is a well-worn carved motif in the wooden door-frame to the end ground-floor room, where the inglenook fireplace has been filled in and replaced by a modern surround, but the large chimney-breast still projects outwards from the rear exterior wall.[127] Most of the rafters and joists in the loft are the original timbers, but some have been renewed. A Mr. Camden carved his name on one of the joists, and another has the inscription: *1847 H. BROWN 24 JUL* on it. The exposed part of the centre chimney-breast shows that it was enlarged at about the same time that the smaller section of it was completed.[184]

In the modernised section of the farmhouse, the gothic windows which have now been replaced by modern ones were found to be of inferior quality to those in the other half of the house, and had a different, smaller wooden framework around them.[183] There is a large cellar beneath this part of the building, and some marks left on the rear wall indicate the position of the old staircase down into it.[127]

Various items of interest have been discovered in and around the farmhouse in recent years, and include one George III halfpenny dated 1806 attached to the underside of a floorboard; a small silver horseshoe, and a frame for a miniature painting, or photograph, from beneath the floor. A French coin was dug up in the front garden, and other articles were uncovered elsewhere in the grounds, including another coin dated 1862 depicting the young Queen Victoria, an old button from a military uniform, some pottery, two pieces of china figurines, and a large brass badge from some kind of machinery.[126]

Parts of the flint walls around the farmhouse can still be seen, and there is a section of a brick and flint wall by the bridle path at the side of the garden. Most of the barns and other farm buildings have disappeared from the farmyard, including one large barn which stood at the end of the bridle way across the smallholdings. It would now be difficult to trace the exact position of the blacksmith's shop shown on Daniel Burrell's map of 1818, because its site is covered over with undergrowth and trees.[127]

DIAGRAM 8.
(not to scale)
Taken from Ordnance
Survey Map of 1896.

LITTLE WOODCOTE FARMHOUSE.

(Woodmansterne Lane)

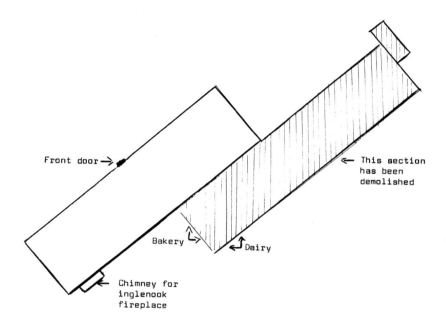

Front door →

This section
has been
demolished

Bakery

Dairy

Chimney for
inglenook
fireplace

(Little Woodcote Lane)

Recently, another part of former Little Woodcote has gained some publicity because of the uncertain future of Queen Mary's Hospital, and the renewed interest in the old enclosure. From the information now available concerning the finds in only a small section of it since the beginning of the present century, it is believed to be one of the most important sites of its kind in Greater London, and the Secretary of State for the Environment has been asked to define it as a Scheduled Ancient Monument.[185]

At Carshalton on the Hill, Stanley House presents a well-kept appearance and is now over one hundred and twenty years old.[150] Its special features are the front porch, with its pillars and decorative wrought-iron balcony; the unusual pattern of the tiles on the roof, which has wide, projecting eaves with modillions, and the small windows in both gable ends. Its tall, Tudor-style chimneys were reduced in height in recent years, and most of these have been cut down to the level of the chimney stacks.

SIR JOHN IWARDBY'S CLAIM TO THE MANORS OF BEDDINGTON, BANDON AND NORBURY AT THE ESCHEATOR OF SURREY'S INQUISITION, FEBRUARY, 1493

(a) Extract from Carew Manuscript 3/5 (Central Library's Archives, Sutton)

John Iwardby and Sanche his wiff claimeth rightful of Richard Carru of the Manor of Bedington and all the lands in Surry sometime Thomas Huscarl. And the Manors of Bandon and Norbury...the said sheir and tenth of rent in Croidon...that Reymond Carru, Regnold Sheffield and John At thorne were seized in fee of part of said manor of Bedyngton and of other lands sometime Thomas Huscarll in Surry, as hit so apperith by Fine made by tween old Nicholas Carru in the 23rd year of King Edward the third and the said Thomas Huscarll. Which Reymond, Regnold and John yave by Dede credibill the said manor of Bedyngton, and all the lands sometime the said Huscarll in Surry to the said Nicholas Carru term of his lyff, the remainder to Nicholas Carru, sonn of the said Nicholas, and to the heirs of his body lawfully begoten...

(b) Carew Manuscript 3/6 (Central Library's Archives, Sutton) being part of the evidence presented on Richard Carew's behalf.

Item: Nicholas Carru grandfather to James Carru purchased serten lands called Gret Farnams contayning 20 aqrs in wod and pastur lying in the beque of Bencham, and Little Farnams contayning 5 aqrs lying ther by the tiled houis. Which lands Jack of Farnam and Juliau his wiff willed that hit shuld be sold and the money payd of to be disposed to reparacion on the Church of Croidon, the which money the said Nicholas Carru payd and hadd the said lands.

Item: The said Nicholas Carru purchased a peis of land of Renns lying next Wodcott contayning 14 aqrs lying upon houis northward, also he purchased 3 aqrs of land in beryfield sometime parish of

Cheihum, and he purchased a peis of land in Walington sometime the half is of St. Thomas in Suthwark lying by the way fro Walton crost to Bedington. And a nather land sometime Thomas Bishop lying by Dymock is land at the croft suthward, and a nather sometime Merton, past al this is held of Dymoke as is the said rete as hit apperith by rentalles etc.

Item: A peis of land in Bedington called Freris aqrs held of the Priory of Merton.

Thes lands rents and tenements was purchased by Foster* at several timis in King Edward third is days as hit apperith by old evidens, which is no parcell of the said John of Bandon. Reginold Foster purchased of William Charrois of Cheihum 2s.4d. of rent of a meis sometime John Gordon of Bandon, and 2 aqrs lying their in the suthfeild, where of one ather is in longefurlonge and tother in Estenord. Also he purchased of him 2s. of rent in Bandon and 2 aqrs their in the suthfeild, one in Longefurlonge and tother in Estnordine. Also the said Foster hadd a reles of Sir Thomas Huscarll of 2s.6d. of rent, one of a feild in Wodcott called Elongefeild lying in the parish of Bedington, and yet the Lord of the Manor of Huscarll oweth to haim a part of 2s.6d. yelding of the said feild. Also the said Foster purchased of John Charlwode and Mable his wiff al the lands that they hadd in Bedyngton, Carshalton and Wodmanston, sometime Feron Momoir and Margret his wiff. Also he purchased of John Waleton 2 aqrs of land at Wodcott by tween the land sometime of John Bordwode and Sabyn his wiff, and Fosters land lying in boith side part of. Also he purchased of the said John of Waleton other 2 aqrs of land at Wodcott lying by tween the land sometime the said John Bordwode and Sabin his wiff. Also Foster purchased of Cristin Atbreke and of Richard Atbreke of Bandon a croft with appurtenances in Bandon lying by tween the mancion their sometime the said Cristin, and a tenement their sometime John Garet on the est part, and a tenement their sometime John Atmede and Richard Grove on the west part. Also the said Foster purchased a feild in Croidon of John of Purley called Frithfeild, which is now Carru is Frith. Also William Foster purchased a croft, 16 aqrs of land and a grove which was sometime Feron Momoir and Margret his wiff. And also 6 aqrs and a half sometime Jone the wiff of Baudwyn Shorgles tavener, and 2 aqrs of land sometime John Reson. Also Foster purchased a tenement in Bandon sometime Richard Atmede and the said Foster yave it to John Baudry and Beatrix his wiff, yelding to the said Foster, his heiris and assignees, 4s. yerly at 4 timis of the yer. Also Foster had of Huscarll 6 aqrs and a half of land, where of 2 aqrs and a half lyeth at Cokkemsthorne by tween Fosters land their and 2 aqrs lyeth at Bynetheburn by tween the land their sometime John Purdom agenst the est and the said Fosters agenst the west. Also Nicholas Carru lett to Farm to Northfolk serten lands that were purchased, that is to say a close in Bandon called Leist Hogge croft of 6 aqrs lying next the hok [oak] by the heath, and a clois their called Gret Thorndon contayning 18 aqrs and a clois lying by Pollards Hill called Walshelery of 5 aqrs eilding yerly to Nicholas Carru and his heiris etc.

As Right Regnerth.

* A shortened form of Forester.

These transcriptions were done by me with some help from staff at the Surrey Record Office. It is as correct as I can make it, but some words and letters may be open to different interpretations.

MC

DISPUTE BETWEEN ANNE BURTON AND SIR FRANCIS CAREW'S TENANT, WILLIAM PAIRE, OVER THE HALF ACRE OF LAND BY THE SHEEPWALK BELONGING TO "WOODCOTT"
CAREW MANUSCRIPT 4/1 (Central Library's Archives, Sutton)

A modernised transcription of:-

34 Interrogations to be ministered on behalf of William Paire, defendant, against Anne Burton, widow, complainant (her son being a royal ward).

1. Do you know the parties, plaintiff and defendant?
2. Did you ever know Sir Nicholas Carew, knight, father of Sir Francis Carew now of Beddington in the county of Surrey, knight; yes or no?
3. Did you know that the said Sir Nicholas Carew was in his lifetime seized in his desmesne as of fee of and in the Manors of Beddington and Bandon in the County of Surrey, and of and in diverse and sundry sheepwalks and sheepsroughs thereunto belonging; yes or no?
4. Do you not also know that the said Sir Nicholas Carew was likewise seized of and in one other capital messuage with appurtenances, and a warren of conyes in Beddington aforesaid, commonly called or known by the names of Woodcott and the Old Lodge? And likewise of and in one other special or severall [separate] sheepwalk or sheepsrough belonging also unto his said Messuage called Woodcott; yes or no?
5. Was not the said sheepwalk or sheepsrough of Woodcott sufficiently and plainly known and bounded out [fenced off] as well from other sheepwalks or sheepsroughs of the said Sir Nicholas Carew of his said Manors of Beddington and Bandon, as also from the sheepwalk or sheepsrough of one Henry Burton of Carshalton, gent.; yes or no?

6. Did not the said sheepwalk or sheepsrough of Woodcott and the bounds thereof by all the time of your remembrance, reach and extend downwards on the north part of the fences onto a certain place called Chamberlaynes Cross, and likewise onto a piece or parcel of arable land of the said Henry Burton's called the fourteen acres, and so from thence westward, along and by the said fourteen acres on to a certain way leading from Wallington towards Reigate; and thence still westward over the same way in and upon one other piece of land of the said Sir Nicholas Carew's containing twenty acres, and lying and next adjoining onto the north part of certain enclosed land of the said Sir Nicholas Carew called the Old Lodge, into one other piece of land of the said Sir Nicholas Carew laying and next adjoining under the south; yes or no?

7. Did you not rightly know, or have you not credibly heard that the said Sir Nicholas Carew, about sixty years now past, did demise and let to farm all his said sheepwalk or sheepsrough of Woodcott as is aforesaid, unto one Henry Burton of Carshalton in the county of Surrey, gent., great-grandfather unto Henry Burton that is now the Queen's Majesty's Ward, for diverse and sundry years to come, and at and for the rent of 26s.8d. by the year; yes or no?

8. Did you not also further know how, at the end of the said Lease, which was about the third year of the reign of the Queen's Majesty that now is, that Sir Francis Carew, knight, son of the said Sir Nicholas Carew, did then also demise and again did let to farm all the said sheepwalk or sheepsrough of Woodcott unto Ellen Burton, widow, grandmother of the said Ward, for the term of twenty-one years and for the yearly rent of 26s.8d. and the keeping of one hundred sheep of the said Sir Francis Carew's and George Butler's; yes or no?

9. Do you not also know that both the said Henry Burton and such as enjoyed the first Lease by and under him, and likewise the said Ellen Burton, did always drive down and kept their sheep in and upon all and every part of these aforesaid twenty acres, which before are said, and set down to, by and adjoining onto the north part of the said Old Lodge, but ever as only tenants and farmers thereof unto the said Sir Nicholas Carew and Sir Francis Carew, and not in their own right, or in the right of any of their own lands, or their own grounds there; yes or no?

10. Did you know, or did you ever hear, that either the said Henry Burton or Nicholas Burton, his son, or the said Ellen Burton, or

any other of the Burtons aforesaid, did challenge or at any time make other title or demands unto a parcel of land, or half acre, lying between the said twenty acres and the said north part of the said Old Lodge, but only by vesture of the Leases and demises from the said Sir Nicholas and Sir Francis Carew as aforesaid, until that about the end and depreciation of the same Leases, and within three years now last past, that one Richard Burton, father of the now Ward, did first begin to make challenge of the same parcel of land, or half acre, as his own freehold land; yes or no?

11. Do you perfectly and certainly know the said parcel of land there in the said enjoyed land is still called the half acre, lying under and between the north part of the said Old Lodge and the said twenty acres of the said Sir Francis Carew; yes or no?

12. Whose hath the inheritance or the fee simple of the same parcel of land, or half acre, been known, or adjudged to be, by all the time of your remembrance?

13. Who hath had the occupation or possession of the same parcel of land, or half acre, and under whom, or by what sufferance or title, have they so occupied or possessed the same by all the time of your remembrance?

14. Did you ever know any marks or bounds, or other severances [fences] or partition on the north side of the said parcel of land, or half acre, that did or might seem to make any appearance of partition or severance between the same and the residue of the said twenty acres of the said Carews; yes or no?

15. Was not the same twenty acres of the Carews which laid under the said north part of the said Old Lodge as aforesaid, always known by the whole time of your remembrance to reach and come by just as far and as high as to the very edge of the said Old Lodge [piece of page missing here] any other lands either of the Burtons or of any other persons lying between [piece of page missing here] twenty acres and the said Old Lodge; yes or no?

16. What trees are now standing, or growing, upon the said parcel of land, or half acre, under the said Old Lodge, and of what age are the same trees?

17. How often have you known the same trees to be lopped or cut?

18. Who did lop or cut the same trees, and by whose appointment or commandment were the same lopped or cut?

19. Do you not verily think that the same trees, or most of them, by reason of their great height and bigness have never been lopped

before such time as Henry Clements did first lop the same; yes or no?

20. To what plans and to whose, or what uses, were the loppings and boughs that were so lopped, or cut, of the same trees, carried or just laid?

21. Did you know, or did you ever hear, that either the said Henry Burton, or Nicholas Burton, or any other of the Burtons, did at any time find fault or any kind of misliking or discontentment either with, or for, the said lopping or cutting of the same trees, or else for the carrying of them away, as is aforesaid; yes or no?

22. Did not you, Henry Clements, rightly remember that at such time as you first lopped the same trees, that the said Henry Burton, the great-grandfather of the now Ward, came that way to his sheepwalk which he held in farm of the Carews, and Bernard his shepherd with him, and seeing you stand so high and so dangerously in lopping of the same trees, did he not come near unto you and say God Speed, and did he not then bid you take your heed that you did not fall, because that he said you stand so high; yes or no?

23. Did he then find fault with you for lopping of the same trees, or did he make any challenge or demands unto the lops, or did he voice any other kind of speech whereby you might, or could, perceive that he want to make any title or demands to the same lops or trees; yes or no?

24. Have not also the said Sir Nicholas Carew and Sir Francis Carew and one Colgat, and other their farmers and tenants of their warren of conyes at Woodcott, always visited there to hunt, and likewise to position their snares for catching of conyes in and upon the said parcel of land, or half acre, under the said Old Lodge; yes or no? And did any of the Burtons ever find fault thereof also; yes or no? Or have the Burtons, or either or any of them claimed any compensation or other kinds of profits upon the said half acre, or only pasture and keeping for their sheep under the vesture of the Leases aforesaid; yes or no?

25. Hath not the said Sir Francis Carew, John William Paire, his tenant, been in full and quiet possession of the same parcel of land, or half acre, under the said Old Lodge ever since the end or depreciation of the said Lease for twenty-one years made unto the said Ellen Burton as aforesaid; yes or no?

26. Have they not daily and weekly driven and kept their sheep

167

thereupon without any title or challenge made thereunto by any of the Burtons, until within these last two or three years that the said Richard Burton, father of the now Ward, first began to challenge and make title to the same; yes or no?

27. Was not the said William Paire, as farmer and tenant unto the said Sir Francis Carew, in full and quiet possession of the same parcel of land, or half acre, at the time of the death of the said Richard Burton; yes or no?

28. Do you not know, or have you not credibly heard, who they were that whilst and during the time that this suit doth depend in the Court of Wards between the said Anne Burton, plaintiff, and the said William Paire, defendant, did secretly, or in the night time, this summer last past, cut and carry away such peason [peas] as the said William Paire had sowed upon the said parcel of land or half acre; yes or no?

29. By whose commandment or appointment did they so fell and carry away the same peason, and which or into what places did they carry and lay the same? And what cart, or horses, had they to carry the same? As you either know or believe of yourself, or else have heard respected thereof by others. Did you not know, or have you not heard that the said Richard Burton in his life time did begin to make challenge and title unto other trees and oaks and loppings of the said Sir Francis Carew's not far distant from the said half acre, where one tree is called the Sottoll Oak? Which trees, do not you know, have always been known and taken to be the Carews'? Yes, and lopped by the Stewards and Officers of the Carews.

30. Do you not think, or have you not heard, that the long possession and occupation by the Burtons of the said sheepwalk by means of the long Leases as aforesaid, did make a great number of people to think that the same was the freehold land of the Burtons, and not owned of by the Carews; yes or no?

31. Do you know that ever the said Henry Burton, or Nicholas Burton, did cut any of the said trees standing upon the said half acre; yes or no?

32. How many, and how often, or how many times, did they lop or cut the same?

33. Was not that lopping or cutting thereof at such and the same time as they farmed and hired the said whole sheepwalk by Lease from the said Sir Nicholas Carew as is aforesaid; yes or no?

34. Did you ever know, or hear, that any of the Burtons did lop any

trees there, either before the time of his said Lease of the sheepwalk began, or else afterwards, after the time of the same Lease was expired and ended; yes or no?

MODERN LOCATIONS

In modern terms, Little Woodcote's largest, triangular-shaped section had its northern boundary along the railway line from approximately three hundred yards west of Park Lane bridge to a point about four hundred yards east of Wallington Station, and its southern apex in Pillory Down, at the bridleway called Grove Lane by the Woodcote Park Golf Course. Since 1829, the following roads have been built on its fields:-

On the eastern side of Woodcote Road (from the railway to Shirley Heights by Woodcote Green).

    Holloway Shott and Smoke Shott: – Ross Parade, Clarendon Road, St. Michael's Road, Ross Road (part), Elgin Road, Stafford Road (up to Elgin Road), Cranley Gardens, Grosvenor Gardens, Onslow Gardens, Blenheim Gardens, Marchmont Road, Avenue Road, Shirley Road, Sandy Hill Road and part of Sandy Lane South (from Sandy Hill Road to Woodcote Green).

On the western side of Woodcote Road (from the railway to Dower Avenue)

    Bowling Green Shott, Wall Shott and No Man's Land: – Beddington Gardens, Shotfield, Holmwood Gardens, Boundary Road (north), Stanley Park Road (north side up to and including Stanley Park High School and grounds).

    Bramble Shott and Catsbrain Shott: – Hawthorn Road, Hawthorne Avenue, Heathdene Road, Brambledown Road, Park Hill Road (up to Brambledown Road), Boundary Road (on east side to Brambledown Road only), Stanley Park Road (south side from Dalmeny Road to Boundary Road only), Dalmeny Road, Mount Park (part), Windborough Road (part), Pine Ridge (part).

    Sandpiece Shott and Vicars Cross Shott: – Stanley Road (part), Stanhope Road (part), Cranfield Road East (part), Southdown Road (part), Fir Tree Grove (part), Queen Mary's Hospital and grounds (part).

    Old Ford, Glebe and Parker's Close: – Briar Lane, Briar Banks,

Bramble Banks, Mount Park (southern end), Mount Way, Mount Close, Boundary Road (southern end on west side by Briar Lane), Pine Ridge (south), Queen Mary's Hospital and grounds (part).

Lawn, Mill Bank Field, Orchard and Barn Field: – Woodcote Avenue (most of both sections), Hall Road, Park Hill Road (from Brambledown Road to Dower Avenue), Glen Road End, Dower Avenue (right-hand side from Woodcote Road only).

Westgate Piece: – East side of Boundary Road (from Brambledown Road to the entrance of the smallholdings), Woodcote Avenue (part of western side of private road), The Woodlands, The Woodend.

Winsome Hill Close: – Part of Queen Mary's Hospital and grounds.

Oak Stubbs Shott and Windborough Hill Shott: – Queen Mary's Hospital and grounds (part), smallholdings (part).

Long Gallop: – Oakhurst Rise, Pine Walk (part), Woodmansterne Road (small part by Oakhurst Rise).

Milton Hill: – Woodmansterne Road (eastern side, approximately from entrance to BIBRA laboratories to last house on smallholdings, on left-hand side from Carshalton Beeches), smallholdings.

Tanner's Piece, Scotch Piece, Pillory Down, Heycott Bottom: – These are used as smallholdings. Little Woodcote Lane (part), Woodmansterne Lane (part).

Maiden's Grave (or Grove): – Little Woodcote Lane (part), Woodmansterne Lane (part), Little Woodcote Cottages, Old Lodge Farm, community hall, factory buildings, old farmyard and part of smallholdings.

It would be difficult to assess accurately the positions of the modern roads on the estate's smaller strips of land shown on the 1818 map.

REFERENCES

1. *The Archaeology of the London Borough of Sutton: an interim survey* by Lesley Adkins, for the South-West London Archaeological Unit, March 1979. Copy in Central Library, Sutton.

2. *Surrey Archaeological Collections*, Volume 75, p.227. "Three later Neolithic discoidal knives from north-east Surrey: with a note on similar examples from the county", by J. Cotton.

3. *Surrey Archaeological Collections*, Volume 77, pp.187-196. "Mesolithic, Neolithic and Bronze Age flint artefacts from Little Woodcote", by Lesley Adkins and Roy Adkins.

4. *Surrey Archaeological Collections*, Volume 20, Stag Field, pp.233-235, Notes IV. "Recent discoveries at Wallington", by George Clinch.

5. *Surrey Archaeological Collections*, Volume 76, pp.11-50. "New research on a late Bronze Age enclosure at Queen Mary's Hospital, Carshalton", by Lesley Adkins and Stuart Needham.

6. *The past – our future*, edited by Clive Orton (Beddington, Carshalton and Wallington Archaeological Society occasional paper 4, 1980), pp.8-12: "Settlement patterns in the area around Beddington, Carshalton and Wallington: an outline of the archaeological evidence", by Lesley Adkins.

7. Information given by Mr. S.A. Bird, Beddington, Carshalton and Wallington Archaeological Society.

8. Adkins, Lesley, and Adkins, Roy. *Archaeological investigation of the Beddington-Mitcham area of opportunity*, 1981. (Seven photocopied pages, plan.) Central Library, Sutton.

9. *Cassell's New English dictionary*; edited by E.A. Baker, Cassell & Co. Ltd., London, 1919.

10. *Surrey Archaeological Collections*, Volume 69, pp.37-45. "Woodcote, or Woodcote Warren, once a City according to Tradition", by K.W. Muckleroy.

11. Manning, Reverend Owen, and Bray, William. *The history and antiquities of the county of Surrey*. 3 vols, 1804-14; facsimile edition, EP Publishing and Surrey County Library, 1974.

12. *Encyclopaedia Britannica*. Encyclopaedia Britannica Ltd., London, 1962.

13. Notes by Nicholas Burnett relating to British Library Manuscript 6167.

14. Aubrey, John. *The natural history and antiquities of the county of Surrey. Begun in the year 1673...* 5 vols, 1718-1719. Facsimile reprint, Kohler & Coombes, Dorking, 1975.

15. Williams, Reverend John. *Historical notes on Wallington*. 1873.

16. *Surrey Life*, September 1976. "Search for a lost City", by Kevin Desmond.

17. "Two Roman coffins from near St. Mary's Church, Beddington", by Lesley Adkins and Roy Adkins, 1984. *Surrey Archaeological Collections*, Volume 75, pp.281-4. (Also published as an offprint.)

18. Surrey Archaeological Society *Bulletin* No.114, 1975, and *Bulletin* No.116, 1975. Extracts in file on archaeological finds at Bandon Hill Cemetery. Central Library, Sutton.

19. Report on further Romano-British finds at Bandon Hill Cemetery by Keith Pryer (typescript). Central Library, Sutton.

20. Surrey taxation returns; fifteenths and tenths. Part (B). Surrey Record Society publications series, Part XXXIII (Volume XI). Butler & Tanner Ltd., Frome and London, for Surrey Record Society, 1932.

21. Jones, A.E. *From medieval manor to London suburb: an obituary of Carshalton*. Published by the author, Carshalton, 1970.

22. Notes by Nicholas Burnett relating to British Library Additional Charters 23020, 23021.

23. British Library Additional Charters 22724, 22942, 22990, 23002, 23050, 23677. Transcripts in Central Library, Sutton.

24. Note of lands in Bandon, not part of the manor of Bandon, and of John Iwardby's title to them, [n.d., c.1494]. Carew manuscript 3/6, Archives of Central Library, Sutton.

25. A Carew family tree compiled by Mrs. J. Carew Richardson. Copy in Central Library, Sutton.

26. Michell, Ronald. *The Carews of Beddington*. London Borough of Sutton Libraries and Arts Services, 1981.

27. Note of grounds of claim of John Iwardby to the manors of Beddington, Bandon and Norbury... [n.d., c.1494]. Carew manuscript 3/5, Archives of Central Library, Sutton.

28. Notes by Nicholas Burnett from the Public Record Office Catalogue of Ancient Deeds, Volume III.

29. Grant of manor of Beddington, 30 August, 1369. Carew manuscript 2163/7/11, Surrey Record Office, Kingston upon Thames.

30. Notes by Mrs. J. Carew Richardson from the Calendars of the Close Rolls, Edward III. Notes in Central Library, Sutton.

31. Notes by Mrs. J. Carew Richardson from the Calendars of the Patent Rolls, Volume 10, Edward III. Notes in Central Library, Sutton.

32. Notes by Mrs. J. Carew Richardson from the Calendars of the Fine Rolls, Edward III. Notes in Central Library, Sutton.

33. Notes by Mrs. J. Carew Richardson from John of Gaunt's Register, Volume 1, Public Record Office. Notes in Central Library, Sutton.

34. Notes by Mrs. J. Carew Richardson from the Calendars of the Charter Rolls, Edward III. Notes in Central Library, Sutton.

35. Notes by Mrs. J. Carew Richardson from the Calendars of the Fine Rolls, Richard II. Notes in Central Library, Sutton.

36. Investigations at Woodcote Hall before and during restoration work by the author and others.

37. Notes by Mrs. J. Carew Richardson from the Calendars of the Fine Rolls, Henry IV. Notes in Central Library, Sutton.

38. Notes by Mrs. J. Carew Richardson from the Calendars of the Fine Rolls, Henry V. Notes in Central Library, Sutton.

39. Notes by Mrs. J. Carew Richardson from the Calendars of the Fine Rolls, Henry VI. Notes in Central Library, Sutton.

40. Notes by Mrs. J. Carew Richardson from the Calendars of the Patent Rolls, Edward IV. Notes in Central Library, Sutton.

41. Notes by Nicholas Burnett relating to British Library Additional Charters 23189, 23193.

42. Notes by Mrs. J. Carew Richardson from the Calendars of the Fine Rolls, Edward IV. Notes in Central Library, Sutton.

43. Notes by Mrs. J. Carew Richardson from the Calendars of the Fine Rolls, Henry VII. Notes in Central Library, Sutton.

44. Notes by Mrs. J. Carew Richardson from the Calendars of the Patent Rolls, Henry VII. Notes in Central Library, Sutton.

45. *Victoria history of the county of Surrey*; edited by H.E. Malden. 4 vols. Archibald Constable & Co. Ltd., 1902. Reprinted for the Institute of Historical Research by Dawsons, London, 1967. Vol.3, pp.223-4.

46. Notes by Mrs. J. Carew Richardson from the Calendars of the

Close Rolls, Henry VII. Notes in Central Library, Sutton.

47. Brayley, Edward W. *A topographical history of Surrey*. Revised edition by Edward Walford, 4 vols, Virtue [1878].

48. 34 interrogatories...concerning a sheep walk at the north of Woodcote Lodge. [n.d., 16/17 century]. Carew manuscript 4/1, Archives of Central Library, Sutton. (See Appendix III)

49. Observations made on visit to Woodcote Hall Cottage by the author.

50. Notes by Mrs. J. Carew Richardson from the Calendars of the Patent Rolls, Henry VIII. Notes in Central Library, Sutton.

51. Notes by Mrs. J. Carew Richardson from Volume IV, Letters and Papers, Foreign and Domestic, Henry VIII. Notes in Central Library, Sutton.

52. Account of Thomas Mabson of rents...[1550]. Carew manuscript 281/2/18. Surrey Record Office, Kingston upon Thames.

53. Notes by Nicholas Burnett from Carew manuscripts 281/2/18, 281/2/19, Surrey Record Office, Kingston upon Thames.

54. Agreement relating to sheepgate and way... 22 May 1561. Carew manuscript 2163/7/20, Surrey Record Office, Kingston upon Thames.

55. Notes by Nicholas Burnett from Carew manuscripts 281/4/24, 281/4/25, Surrey Record Office, Kingston upon Thames.

56. Carshalton Court Rolls, manuscript transcription in archives of Central Library, Sutton.

57. Notes by Mrs. J. Carew Richardson from Calendars of State Papers, 1547-1580. Notes in Central Library, Sutton.

58. Cockburn, J.S., editor. *Calendar of assize records: Surrey indictments, Elizabeth I*. HMSO, 1980.

59. Bentham, Reverend Thomas. *The History of Beddington*. John Murray, London, 1923.

60. *Victoria history of the county of Surrey*; edited by H.E. Malden. 4 vols. Archibald Constable & Co. Ltd., 1902; reprinted for the Institute of Historical Research by Dawsons, London, 1967.

61. *Surrey Archaeological Collections*, Volume 77, pp.181-186. "Queen Elizabeth I and the Croydon horse race, with a check-list of the Queen's visits to Croydon", by Marion Calthorpe.

62. Notes by Nicholas Burnett from Carew manuscript 218/1/1, p.5. Surrey Record Office, Kingston upon Thames.

63. *Surrey Archaeological Collections*, Volume 7, pp.126-151 (p.143). "Notes on the parish and church of Carshalton", by Thomas

Milbourn, Architect.

64. *Surrey hearth tax, 1664: being an alphabetical list of entries in the record*; edited by C.A.F. Meekings and with a preliminary note by Hilary Jenkinson, 1940. (Surrey Record Society publications series, Vol. XVII serial publication nos. 41 and 42). Central Library, Sutton.

65. Observations made on visits to West Lodge by the author and others.

66. *Surrey Archaeological Collections*, Volume 16, pp.1-27 (p.6). "Notes on the manor and parish of Woodmansterne", by F.A.H. Lambert, F.S.A.

67. Mortimer, Roger. *The history of the Derby Stakes*, second edition, Michael Joseph Ltd., London, 1973.

68. Notes by Mrs. J. Carew Richardson from the will of Sir Nicholas Carew of Beddington, knight (probate – March, 1688). Notes in Central Library, Sutton.

69. Copy deed of appointment of Dame Eliz. Carew and Sir Nic. Hacket Carew...20 Jan. 1740. Carew manuscript 1/1, archives of Central Library, Sutton.

70. Copy of deeds of part of Little Woodcote Estate. Central Library, Sutton.

71. Jones, A.E. *An illustrated directory of old Carshalton*. Published by the author, Carshalton, 1973.

72. Copy will of Sir William Scawen. Surrey Record Office, Kingston upon Thames.

73. Note supplied by Mrs. M.J. Hamilton-Bradbury on an Indenture of Lease dated 1st June, 1719, between Sir William Scawen and Joseph Eyles, in the Minet Library, Lambeth.

74. Jones, A.E. *The Story of Carshalton House*. London Borough of Sutton Libraries and Arts Services, 1980.

75. Fleming, Laurence, and Grove, Alan. *The English Garden*. Appendix 2, p.241. Michael Joseph Ltd., London, 1979.

76. Copy will of Sir Thomas Scawen, Public Record Office, London.

77. *Surrey Archaeological Collections*, Volume 3, pp.193-207 (p.205). "Further remarks on some of the ancient inns of Southwark", by W.H. Hart, Esq., F.S.A.

78. 'The Peatling Papers'. An unpublished work relating to the local history of Carshalton, compiled by Dr. A.V. Peatling c.1902-1922. Original in the archives of Central Library, Sutton, 14 vols. with index. Photocopies in Sutton, Carshalton and Wallington Libraries.

79. Peel, Edward. *Cheam School from 1645*. The Thornhill Press, Gloucester, 1974 (on behalf of the Cheam School Association).

80. *The Lady's Magazine*, August 1775. Copy of extract in Central Library, Sutton.

81. The Court Book for the manors of Ewell and Cuddington with, at the back of the book, the manors of East and West Cheam, 1725-1765. 2238/10/171, Surrey Record Office, Kingston upon Thames.

82. Brightling, George B. *Some particulars relating to the history and antiquities of Carshalton...* 1st edition 1872. 2nd edition 1882. Facsimile reprint of 2nd edition with added index, London Borough of Sutton Libraries and Arts Services, 1978.

83. Notes by Mrs. M.J. Hamilton-Bradbury from *British Botanical and Horticultural Literature, before 1800*, by Blanche Henrey. Oxford, 1975 (pp.450 & 455), in the Royal Horticultural Society's Library, Old Hall, Vincent Square, London.

84. Namier, Sir Lewis, and Brooke, John. *The history of Parliament: The House of Commons 1754-1790*. 3 vols. HMSO, 1964.

85. Edwards, James. *Companion from London to Brighthelmston*, 2nd edition (1801). Extract in Central Library, Sutton.

86. Notes by Mrs. M.J. Hamilton-Bradbury from two volumes of *Catalogues of Picture Sales in England, 1711-1759*. Also additional information on card index headed: SCAWEN, Thomas. Victoria & Albert Museum Library (restricted material).

87. Notes by Mrs. M.J. Hamilton-Bradbury from two volumes of *Catalogues of Picture Sales in England, 1711-1759*, Volume II, p.109. Victoria & Albert Museum Library (restricted material).

88. Barrett, C.R.B. *Surrey: highways, byways and waterways*. Bliss & Co., London, 1895.

89. Carshalton poor rate books. Archives of Central Library, Sutton.

90. Copy will of William Scawen. Public Record Office, London.

91. *Surrey Archaeological Collections*, Volume 39, pp.82-103 (p.103). "Answers made to the visitation of Dr. Willis, the Bishop of Winchester, from the parishes in Surrey, excluding the peculiars of Canterbury, 1724-25". Abridged and annotated from the manuscript formerly at Farnham Castle and now in the Cathedral Library, Winchester, by H.E. Malden, M.A.

92. Pybus Deeds. Indentures of Bargain and Sale, 7th/8th October, 1771, between William Scawen and Edmund Sanxay. P 3/33, archives of Central Library, Sutton.

93. Marshall, Charles John. *A History of the Old Villages of Cheam*

and Sutton... Cryer's Library, Cheam, 1936.

94. Pybus Deeds. Indentures of Lease and Release, 29th/30th September, 1684. P 3/22, archives of Central Library, Sutton.

95. Pybus Deeds. Copy of the Reverend Henry Day's will. P 3/23, archives of Central Library, Sutton.

96. Information supplied by the late Leslie Boakes.

97. Rocque's map of Surrey, 1768.

98. Pybus Deeds. Cheam House Indentures (including plans). P 3/1-139, archives of Central Library, Sutton.

99. Pybus Deeds. Extract from the Reverend Daniel Sanxay's will. Surrey Record Office, Kingston upon Thames.

100. *Surrey Archaeological Collections*, Volume 7, pp.126-151 (p.147). "Notes on the parish and church of Carshalton" by Thomas Milbourn, Architect.

101. Ingram, D. *A strict and impartial enquiry into the cause and death of the late William Scawen, Esquire, of Woodcote Lodge in Surrey, ascertaining from medical evidence against Jane Butterfield, the impossibility of poison having been given him.* T. Cadell, 1777. An original copy at Bourne Hall Library, Ewell. Photocopy in the Central Library, Sutton.

102. Land tax books for Beddington, 1780 onwards. QS 6/7. Surrey Record Office, Kingston upon Thames.

103. Indenture of Feof(f)ment and Release in Fee in four parts for securing £40,000 and interest, dated 20th April, 1779, between the Rt. Hon. Henry, Earl Bathurst, Robert Scawen, Robert Drummond and Charles Bragge, esquires (trustees) of the first part; James Scawen esquire of the second part, the Rt. Hon. Richard Rigby of the third part, and Richard Barnes, gentleman, of the fourth part. 173/1/3. Surrey Record Office, Kingston upon Thames.

104. Notes by Mrs. M.J. Hamilton-Bradbury from Deed of Appointment, 1st August, 1787, from James Scawen "late of Carshalton, Surrey, now of Maidwell, Northants.", appointing Alan Chambre of Grays Inn as trustee of C.F. Wintour's marriage settlement, in the room of the said J. Scawen. The Minet Library, Lambeth.

105. Map of Surrey c. 1786 attributed to John Cary. Archives of Central Library, Sutton.

106. Notes by Mrs. J. Carew Richardson from the will of Sir Nicholas Hacket Carew. Notes in Central Library, Sutton.

107. Notes by Mrs. M.J. Hamilton-Bradbury from abstracts in the calendar of Surrey Deeds, No.4026 (1773) copy of a Court Roll. The Minet Library, Lambeth.

108. Notes by Mrs. J. Carew Richardson from the will of Catherine Carew. Notes in Central Library, Sutton.

109. Carshalton Vestry Minutes. LG 1/1-2, LG 5/1/1, LG 15/16, archives of Central Library, Sutton.

110. Copy will of John Durand. Public Record Office, London.

111. Spear, Percival. *The Oxford history of modern India, 1740-1975*. Second edition, Oxford University Press, 1978.

112. Barrett, C.R.B. *The Trinity House of Deptford Strand*. Lawrence & Bullen, London, 1893.

113. *Harmsworth's Universal Encyclopaedia*; edited by J.A. Hammerton. 9 vols. The Amalgamated Press Ltd., London, 1920.

114. Mylne, Robert. *Robert Mylne, architect and engineer, 1733 to 1811*; [diaries; edited, with an introduction, by A.E. Richardson]. B T Batsford, London, 1955.

115. Cox, Millard. *Derby: the life and times of the twelfth Earl of Derby, Edward Smith Stanley (1752-1834)*. J.A. Allen, London, 1974.

116. *Victoria history of the county of Worcester*; edited by J.W. Willis-Bund and William Page. 4 vols. Archibald Constable & Co. Ltd., 1901. Reprinted for the Institute of Historical Research by Dawsons, London, 1971.

117. Carshalton parish registers. Surrey Record Office, Kingston upon Thames.

118. Hassell, John. *Picturesque Rides and Walks, with excursions by water, thirty miles round the British Metropolis*. Volume 1, 1817. 2 vols., F.P., London, 1817-18. British Library. Microfilmed extract in Central Library, Sutton.

119. Garrow, D.W. *The history and antiquities of Croydon...* Croydon, 1818.

120. Steinman, G. *A history of Croydon*. London, 1833.

121. Beddington parish registers. Surrey Record Office, Kingston upon Thames. Transcript and index in the Central Library, Sutton.

122. Copy will of John Hodsdon Durand. Public Record Office, London.

123. Woodcote Hall before 1912 as described by the late Mrs. Patricia Clark.

124. Author's and author's late parents' memories of Woodcote Hall in 1935/6.

125. Survey map of Little Woodcote by Daniel Burrell (1818). Surrey Record Office, Kingston upon Thames.

126. Information supplied by the owner of 2, Little Woodcote Cottages.

127. Investigations at Little Woodcote Cottages by author and others.

128. Berry, William. *Surrey* (County Genealogies). Sherwood, Gilbert and Piper, London, 1837.

129. Ledger G (p.144), Wedgwood Museum. Tracing of entry in Central Library, Sutton.

130. Extracts from the *Wallington Times* and the *Daily Express*, 10th March, 1910. Central Library, Sutton.

131. Information supplied by Maidstone library from contemporary local newspapers.

132. *Surrey Archaeological Collections*, Volume 43, pp.1-15 (p.13). "Hunting in Surrey", by the Earl of Onslow, P.C., F.S.A.

133. Plans on copy deeds of The Oaks. Archives of Central Library, Sutton.

134. Ordnance Survey map, 2nd edition, twenty-five inches to the mile. 1896.

135. Valuation of the Hamlet of Wallington in the Parish of Beddington for the purpose of making an equal parish rate assessment. 1806.

136. Copy will of John Hassell Durand. Public Record Office, London.

137. Public Record Office, London.

138. Copy of title deeds of Woodcote Hall with plans, in author's possession.

139. Lysons, Daniel. *The environs of London: being an historical account of the towns, villages and hamlets within twelve miles of the capital.* 1st edition, 5 vols., 1792-1800, supplement 1811.

140. *Victoria history of the county of Essex.* 4 vols. Archibald Constable & Co. Ltd., Westminster, 1903. Reprint in 8 vols.; edited by W.R. Powell, published for the Institute of Historical Research by the Oxford University Press, 1966.

141. Copy will of William Turner. Public Record Office, London.

142. *Two hundred and fifty years of map-making in the county of Surrey.* A collection of reproductions of printed maps published between the years 1579-1823 with introductory notes by William Ravenhill. Harry Margary, Lympne Castle, Kent, 1974. *contains* Map of the County of Surrey from an Actual Survey made in the years 1822 and 1823 by C. & I. Greenwood, London. Central Library, Sutton.

143. *The Greville Memoirs, 1814-1860*; edited by Lytton Strachey and Roger Fulford. Macmillan & Co., London, 1938.

144. Lease (contract for sale) between the Rt. Hon. Edward, Earl of Derby and Sir Charles Edward Grey, 3rd February, 1834, and conveyance and deed of covenant between the same parties, 4th February, 1834. Copy deeds of The Oaks, archives of Central Library, Sutton.
145. Tithes, rents and charges book for Beddington, 1839. Surrey Record Office, Kingston upon Thames.
146. Copy of census returns for 1841. Central Library, Sutton.
147. Beddington poor rate books, 1839-1841. Surrey Record Office, Kingston upon Thames.
148. Copy of census returns for 1851. Central Library, Sutton.
149. *Encyclopaedia Britannica.* Encyclopaedia Britannica Ltd., London, 1896.
150. Deeds of Stanley House, with plans, in possession of Mrs. M.E. Reynolds (née Hosker).
151. Ordnance Survey map, 1st edition, twenty-five inches to the mile. 1868.
152. Copy of census returns for 1871. Central Library, Sutton.
153. Copy of census returns for 1881. Central Library, Sutton.
154. *Pile's Beddington, Carshalton and Wallington Directories*, published by William Pile Ltd., 1876-1937. Central Library, Sutton.
155. *Surrey Archaeological Collections*, Volume 7, pp.xxxiii-xxxix (p.xxxvii). Reports of proceedings of a meeting of Surrey Archaeological Society at the Public Hall, Croydon, Wednesday 14th March, 1877.
156. Information supplied by the author's late parents.
157. Information supplied by Miss Joyce Breadon.
158. Letter and map of Little Woodcote Estate, 1898. Imperial Property Development Company Limited. LG 6/8/7/18-19, archives of Central Library, Sutton.
159. *All our yesterdays: a pictorial record of the London Borough of Sutton over the last century*, compiled by Ian Bradley, June Broughton and Douglas Cluett. Sutton Libraries and Arts Services, 1977.
160. Carshalton poor rate book 1812-1821. LG 15/20/4, archives of Central Library, Sutton.
161. Information supplied by Mrs. Norah Hartland (former tenant at Woodcote Hall).
162. Beddington, Carshalton and Wallington Archaeological Society,

Occasional Newsletter No.17, February 1981. Article in the series 'Old inhabitants' recollections of the Beddington, Carshalton and Wallington area'.

163. Information supplied by the owners of Mr. Mayer's house in 1982.

164. Ordnance Survey map, 3rd edition, twenty-five inches to the mile, 1913.

165. Festing, Sally. *The story of lavender*. London Borough of Sutton Libraries and Arts Services, 1982.

166. Information supplied by Mrs. M.E. Reynolds (née Hosker).

167. Information supplied by Mr. J.S. Waites.

168. Copy deeds of 25, Pine Ridge, Carshalton, in possession of author.

169. Information supplied by the late Reverend Costin L. Densham.

170. Information supplied by Mrs. Hylda Boakes.

171. Leslie Boakes's scrap book in possession of Mrs. Hylda Boakes.

172. Information supplied by Mr. J. Vinn.

173. Information supplied by Mrs W.C. Bond (former tenant at Woodcote Hall).

174. Information supplied by Mr. H.G.W. Hosking (former tenant at Woodcote Hall).

175. Information supplied by Mrs. G.C.M. de Koning (former tenant at Woodcote Hall).

176. Information supplied by Mrs. F.C. Bridle (former tenant at Woodcote Hall).

177. Information supplied by the late Mr. Farren of Farren Estates Ltd.

178. Information supplied by Mr. David Jackson.

179. Investigation of the large cellar at Woodcote Hall with Mr. J. Henderson of the Chelsea Speleological Society, and others.

180. Investigation of the lofts over the eastern front section of Woodcote Hall by Messrs. Douglas Cluett and Barry Weston.

181. Information supplied by Miss S. Theakstone.

182. Paintings of West Lodge by Miss Sheila Ellis. Archives of Central Library, Sutton.

183. Information supplied by Mr. E. Fuller (Little Woodcote Cottages).

184. Investigation of the loft over 2, Little Woodcote Cottages by Messrs. Douglas Cluett and John Phillips.

185. *Sutton Advertiser*, 4th September, 1986.

186. *A letter to Mr. Sanxay, Surgeon, in Essex Street. Occasioned by his very singular conduct, in the prosecution of Miss Butterfield, who was tried at the Assizes at Croydon, Aug. 19, 1775, for poisoning the*

late William Scawen, Esq., of Woodcote-Lodge, in the County of Surrey, and honourably acquitted. G. Kearsly, London, 1775. Copy in Central Reference Library, Croydon.

187. *The trial of Jane Butterfield for the wilful murder of William Scawen, Esq., at the assizes held at Croydon for the County of Surrey on Saturday the 19th August, 1775, before the Right Honourable Sir Sydney Stafford Smythe, Knt., Lord Chief Baron of His Majesty's Court of Exchequer. Published by permission of the Judge. Taken in shorthand by Joseph Gurney and William Blanchard.* W. Owen & G. Kearsly, London, 1775. Copy in Central Reference Library, Croydon.

188. Visit to Woodcote Hall in November, 1987.

INDEX

Numbers in **bold** type denote illustrations

Brambledown Road, 120,123,127,
132
Braybrook, *Sir* Edward, 139
Brendwode, John **see** Bordwode
Briar Banks, Carshalton, 12
Briar Lane, Carshalton, 12
Bridle Way (Boundary Road), 19,
50,115,127,156
Bradford, William, 32
Broadhead, Theodore, 99
Broadway, The, Cheam, 62
Brocklesby, *Dr.*, 70
Bromfield, *Mr.*, 70
Brooke Bond & Co. Ltd., 136
Brown, *Major-Gen.* Montague, 123
Brown, *Capt.* Thomas, 96,99,104,
106
Bryan, *Sir* Francis, 34,36
Bryan, *Sir* Thomas, 34
Buck, *Mr.* R.S. and *Mrs.* L.J.,
130,131
'Bullens Closes', 54
Burrell, Daniel, **10-11**,115,145,**146**,
147,149,151,160
Burton, Anne, 48,164,168
Charles, 50
Ellen, 45,48,165,167
Harry D., 135,136
Henry *d.1543*, 37,45,48,164,165,
167,168
Henry *d.1630*, 49
Sir Henry *d.1647*, 48,49-50
Mabel, 48
Nicholas, 45,165,167,168
Richard, 45,48,166,168
Butler, George, 42,45,165
Butterfield, Jane, **46**,**47**,60,64,65-80
Byne, Charles, 52
Byne, Edmund, 53
Byne, Henry, 84,97,99,104

Camden, William, 13,16,17,21
Cantwell, Joseph, 69
Carew, Carru, Carreu family,
Ann, 29
Anne (*née* Boteler), 52
Anne Hacket, 52
Sir Benjamin Hallowell, 111,112
Catherine, 53,82
Charles Hallowell, 112,115

Charles Hallowell Hallowell, 115
Elizabeth *b.1688*, 52
Elizabeth *d.1752*, 53
Elizabeth (*née* Bryan), 34,36,
37,39
Elizabeth (*née* Hacket), 52,53
Sir Francis *d.1611*, 36,39,42,45,
48,49,164,165,166,167,168
Sir Francis *d.1649*, 49,50
Sir Francis *d.1689*, 50,52
James, 29,32
Jane, 50,52
Justiniana, 50
Katherine (*née* Martin), 53
Margaret, 34
Sir Nicholas, *Baron*,
of Moulsford, 23
Nicholas *d.1390*, 24,25,161
Nicholas *d.1432*, 25,27,161,163
Nicholas *d.1458*, 27,28
Nicholas *d.1466*, 28-29, 33
Nicholas *d.c1484*, 28,29
Sir Nicholas K.G. *ex.1539*, 33,34,
35,36,37,39,164,165,166,167,168
Sir Nicholas *d.1688*, 50,52
Nicholas *d.1721*, 50,52
Sir Nicholas *1st Bt.*, *d.1727*, 52
Sir Nicholas (Throckmorton), 49
Sir Nicholas (Hacket) *2nd Bt.*,
d.1762, 52,53,82
Philippa, 50,82
Reymond, 23,24,161
Richard, 50,52
Sir Richard *d.1520*, 29,32,33,34,
36,161
Richard Gee, 82,110,112
Susan, 50
Susannah (*née* Incham), 50,52
Thomas, 24
Master William, 23,24
Carleton, Edward, 54
Carshalton, 34,37,**40**,**41**,45,48,50,
52,54,**55**,56,57,58,60,65,81,82,
84,**88**,99,103,108,112,114,123,162
cricket bowl, **71**,102,108
cricket team, 102
manorial court, 98,106
Carshalton House
(St. Philomena's), 54,
63,99,102,140

East India Company, 82,84,85,91, 96,110

East Lodge (to Woodcote Lodge/ Hall), 98,119,120,127,130

Edgcumbe, *Lord (Admiral)*, 85

Edward III, *King*, 21,24,25

Edward VI, *King*, 39

Edward VII, *King*, 130

Elgin Road, Wallington, 125

Elizabeth I, *Queen*, 48,49

Emor (servant to William Scawen), 68,69

Epsom, Surrey, 36,50,60,84,91

Erle, Robert, 68,69

Ethersey, Elizabeth, 111

Evelyn, John, 16

Ewell Road, Cheam, 62

Eyles, Joseph, 56

Fane, *10th Earl of Westmorland*, 85-6

Farm Lane, Purley, 17

Farmer, Edward, 61

Farrer, William, 82

Fellowes, *Sir* John, 54

Fielding, Henry, 65

Fielding, *Sir* John, 65,80

Finlay Hill, *Messrs.*, 128,130,135, 156

Fir Tree Grove, Carshalton, 130,139

Fitzherbert, Richard, 32

Fling, Mary, 58,60,64,72,80,81

Flying bombs, 140-141

Forester, John, 20,21
    Reginald, 21,27,31,162-3
    Roger, 21
    William, 21,162

Foster *see* Forester

Fountain, *Dr.* John, 82

Frag', Baldr', 20

Freris (Freres) Acres, 162

Gale, Thomas, 16,21

Gale, William Alfred, 116,118

Gale Terrace, Carshalton, 116,141

Garden Hall Cottage, 135,141,142

Garet, John, 162

Gaynesford, John, 32

Gee, Anne Paston, 110,111

Gee, William, 82

George V, *King*
    coronation celebrations, **2**,127

Glenge, William le, 19

Godfrey, *Dr.*, 74

Goodall, Elizabeth (*née* Durand), 96,104,106,107

Goodall, John, 106

Gordon, John, 162

Grace, John *senior*, 107

Greenwich, 34,37
    Hospital 87

Greater Woodcote, 61,82,103,111, 112,138

Green Wrythe Lane, Carshalton, 90

Grene (Gren), Rogero and Waltero ate, 20

Grey, *Sir* Charles Edward, 112

Greyhound Inn, Carshalton, **55**,86, 87,98,102,106,108

Greyhound Inn, Sutton, **63**,106

Grosvenor Square, London, 87, 102,104

Grove, Richard, 162

Hacket, Elizabeth, 52,53

Hacket, *Revd.* John, 61

Hall, Eric, 131-132
    John, 32
    Jane and Richard, 92

Harben, Henry, 99

Hart, Charlotte Maria, 106,107,108

Hartley, *Mr.*, 127

Hassell, John, 92
    Martha *see* Durand, Martha (*née* Hassell)
    Mary, 92

Hastingts, *Lord*, 131

Hawthorn Road, Wallington, 123

Headley, Surrey, 56,57,60

Hearth Tax, 50,61

Heathdene Road, Wallington, 123

Henry VIII, *King*, 33,34,36,37,39

Herb cultivation, **75**,130

Herron, Roger, 32

Heycott Bottom, 138

Higgins, *Dr.*, 68,74

Hill, Alexander, 128,131
    George Finlay, 128,130,131,135, 142
    John, 131,135